I'VE NEVER UNDERSTOOD HOW an expositor who has immersed himself in the biblical text could preach a dull sermon, but I realize that many do—so many, in fact, that expository preaching has acquired a bad reputation in some circles. No wonder. Dry, passionless preaching and murky, technical jargon have ruined countless expository sermons. It doesn't have to be that way. In fact, as Byron Yawn points out so powerfully in this book, good expository preaching should never be dry or merely academic. The faithful expositor's duty entails much more than sound exegesis and symmetrical outlines. The delivery of the sermon is crucial. Zeroing in, especially on qualities like clarity, simplicity, and passion, Byron hits all the right notes. Every preacher who wants to be an effective expositor should read this book and take it to heart.

   —DR. JOHN MACARTHUR
    Pastor-Teacher, Grace Community Church
    President The Master's College and Seminary

IN OUR AGE OF CELEBRITY PREACHING, ordinary preachers can begin to think that style ultimately determines whether preaching is great or not. Byron Yawn has provided a needed and helpful corrective by showing that what makes preaching great, instead, are three qualities: clarity, depth, and passion. The preachers he interviews are among the greats of our day, to be sure. But what makes them great as preachers are these three qualities that all good preaching should have, that your and my preaching may have. Experienced preachers, as well as those just starting out, will benefit much from getting clear on what matters most in our preaching, and Well-Driven Nails will help much in pointing us all in the right direction.

   —DR. BRUCE A. WARE
    Professor of Christian Theology
    The Southern Baptist Theological Seminary
    Louisville, KY

THROUGH INTERVIEWING THREE of the most notable preachers of 21st-century North America in areas of their giftedness—Dr. John MacArthur on clarity, Dr. R. C. Sproul on simplicity, and Dr. John Piper on sincerity—this fascinating book is a tonic and help for every Spirit-anointed preacher who wants to journey beyond seminary mediocrity to find liberation in exegesis, freedom in the pulpit and, above all, discovery of his own voice in faithfully expounding God's Word in and out of season. If you want to grow in pulpit authenticity and freedom from being a clone in preaching, read this gripping book prayerfully and slowly. You won't be sorry.

   —DR. JOEL R. BEEKE
    President of Puritan Reformed Theological Seminary
    Grand Rapids, MI

How wonderfully refreshing to read Byron's challenge to pastors, teachers, and preachers to "find their own voice" to effectively proclaim the Gospel and the truths of God's Word. His emphasis on clarity, simplicity, and passion is right on. But this isn't just for the professionals. It's for church leaders and laity alike...for all of us as Christ-followers. We're all instructed to always be ready to explain the reason for the Hope that is in us. And today—more than ever—we need men, women and youth who re-claim our responsibility to know the Scriptures, understand what God is saying, find our "voice" too, and speak intelligently with Biblical accuracy and cultural relevancy to our friends and neighbors and in the market square.

—BILL ANDERSON
Executive Mentor & Consultant to CEOs
Former President Christian Booksellers Association
Colorado Springs, CO

Predictable surprises should not surprise us at all, but they do. So it was when Byron Yawn joined thousands of fellow preachers who feel their well has run dry and need to discover why. So the search focuses on how to do exegesis of Scripture, how to do preaching, how to do illustrations, how to do almost anything, only to discover that preaching excellence starts with the preacher. Excellence is an intrinsic matter more than a process. This is an excellent book, not only for preachers who strive for excellence in preaching, but also for all listeners who strive for excellence in listening. That should include all of us, shouldn't it?

—DR. V. GILBERT BEERS, PHD, THD
Former President Scripture Press Ministries,
Former Editor Christianity Today
Author of more than 150 bestselling titles
Graduate, Northwestern University; Northern Baptist Theological Seminary

Here is a must read book for every preacher who seeks to find his own individual voice and develop his own personal style in the pulpit. Each preacher is a one of a kind instrument, uniquely gifted by God, to proclaim His glory. This book will help guide you to be that preacher.

—DR. STEVEN LAWSON
Senior Pastor, Christ Fellowship Baptist Church
Mobile, AL
Graduate, Texas Tech University, Dallas Theological Seminary, and Reformed Theological Seminary

As a shepherd and leader, Byron effectively communicates confidence in the truth without taking himself too seriously. Since I have known Byron, he has served my young family sacrificially and has been transparent as both a pastor and a friend. This off season, his transformed preaching set me on fire for the Gospel, and reading this book makes me excited to find my own voice in Christ to courageously lead my family every week!

—BEN ZOBRIST
Tampa Bay Rays Super Utility Player
Graduate, Dallas Baptist University
Member, Community Bible Church
Nashville, TN
www.cbcnnashville.org

Every Sunday, my pastor opens the Bible, and standing before the spectacle of God's glorious grace presented there, says, "Get a load of this!" Byron's preaching is leadership. It's leadership because it's not only an exposition of the scripture but an exposition of his own soul caught in the grip of the cross. This book is the same way—a transparent self-examination that will show the frustrated preacher how to find his voice, and so to lead his people.

—DOUG SEARLE
Elder, Community Bible Church, Nashville, TN
Graduate, University of Washington, Seattle, WA
Th.M. Dallas Theological Seminary, Dallas, TX
www.cbcnnashville.org

Few can ask the right questions the way Byron can. He not only helps us know what to ask regarding the issues of preaching, but he leads us to answers which strike at the heart of the craft and are derived from experience. Well-Driven Nails is a great gift from the Lord Jesus through his servant Byron Yawn. Take up and read.

—PATRICK ABENDROTH
Senior Pastor
Omaha Bible Church, Omaha, NE
Graduate, University of Nebraska, Lincoln and The Master's Seminary
www.omahabiblechurch.org/north

Well-Driven Nails

The Power of Finding Your Own Voice

Well-Driven Nails

The Power of Finding Your Own Voice

BYRON FORREST YAWN

Ambassador International

GREENVILLE, SOUTH CAROLINA & BELFAST, NORTHERN IRELAND

www.ambassador-international.com

Well-Driven Nails

The Power of Finding Your Own Voice

Printed in the United States of America

ISBN: 978-1-935507-33-8

Cover Design & Page Layout by David Siglin of A&E Media

AMBASSADOR INTERNATIONAL
Emerald House
427 Wade Hampton Blvd.
Greenville, SC 29609, USA
www.ambassador-international.com

AMBASSADOR BOOKS
The Mount
2 Woodstock Link
Belfast, BT6 8DD, Northern Ireland, UK
www.ambassador-international.com

The colophon is a trademark of Ambassador

Patti M. Hummel
President & Agent
THE BENCHMARK GROUP LLC, Nashville, TN
www.benchmarkgrouppublishers.com

This book was edited by:
Vicki Huffman, VP/Senior Editor
THE BENCHMARK GROUP LLC, NASHVILLE, TN
benchmarkgroup2@aol.com

To my wife Robin

The only woman I've ever loved.

In addition to being a wise man, the Preacher
also taught the people knowledge; and he pondered,
searched out and arranged many proverbs. The Preacher
sought to find delightful words and to write words of
truth correctly. The words of wise men are like goads,
and masters of these collections are like **well-driven nails**;
they are given by one Shepherd.

ECCLESIASTES 12:9-11

Table of Contents

Introduction

Explanations: Where It Started

As the saying goes, "If ministry doesn't work out, continue your education." In my case, ministry was working out fine. My problem was delivery in preaching. Ten years into my experience of consecutive exposition I found myself in a rut. A rut which was as equally hard to explain as it was to get out of. In order to shake things up and hone my skill as an expositor, I entered a D.Min. program focusing on *Expository Preaching*. I set out to face what I soon discovered was a common struggle for many biblical expositors—*delivery*.

Many of my fellow students and I shared a mutual frustration—our preaching lacked an authentic dynamic. To one degree or another, each of us needed some life breathed into our preaching. The very reason most of us were there together. It was reassuring to meet others at a similar stage of their ministry with a similar need—breaking through in their preaching and delivery. It was a two-year "you're not crazy" session. It was a support group for preachers. "Hello, my name is Byron, and I'm boring."

So there we were, reminding ourselves of the glory of preaching, resurrecting our language skills and desperately seeking to rejuvenate our delivery. The elephant in the room was ever present and hard to ignore.

Why is it those committed to biblical exegesis and expository preaching struggle with delivery? Is it necessary for expository preaching to be predictably mechanical, cerebral and dull? How do we get over the "hump" without compromising biblical authority, jumping on the band wagon of the latest trend or sounding like sanctified life coaches? Where is the balance between exegesis and delivery? This was the *Gordian knot* most of us had come to untie. Even the faculty recognized the challenge of effectively teaching the relationship of scholarship and dynamic. Personally, I struggled to move from what I would describe as *expository teaching* to *expository preaching*. It became a personal quest.

The idea of interviewing preachers occurred to me well into the second year of my coursework during a specific class. The speaker for the two-day seminar on narratives, an adjunct professor, was a well-known pastor and author from the area who had nearly twenty-five years of preaching experience.[1] On the first day, he processed through his syllabus like some sort of machine. It was all helpful information; I even remember some of it. On the second day, I experienced the best lecture of the entire program. He set his binder aside and talked shop with us. He fielded question after question. His answers combined biblical authority with practical wisdom. It was not theoretical, but practical.

That is when it occurred to me: *What if I could sit down with all the preachers I most admire and do the same thing? Those preachers who seem to have found the balance in their own preaching. What if I could pinpoint those qualities in areas where I most need to improve, find the expositors who best exemplify them and pick their brains?*

So that's what I did.

I selected three specific areas I knew were at the root of the problem: *Clarity*, *Simplicity* and *Passion*. I then looked to those men who best represented these particular characteristics. During the research phase of the project, I interacted with a wide selection of preachers from all sorts of contexts. Large churches and small. Vast experience and limited. When it came to writing, I focused on three specific and well-known preachers around whom I would develop the core arguments. John MacArthur for *Clarity*. R.C. Sproul for *Simplicity*. John Piper for *Passion*.

Going in, I knew the solution to my problem was not a simple adjustment in mechanics. I had no interest in pursuing those aspects of preaching which were readily available in most works on homiletics.

---

1   Michael Fabarez, *Preaching That Changes Lives*, (Thomas Nelson: Nashville, 2002).

What I was after wasn't in a book or a course on the subject. The challenge was much deeper than a table of contents. Furthermore, I was not about to give my preaching over to all the haranguing for "relevance" and instant application because I completely disagree with that perspective. I did not need better power-point or enhanced graphics. I was not looking to dumb down my preaching as much as I was seeking to elevate God in the minds of people through it.

What if I could sit down with all the preachers I most admire...those preachers who seem to have found the balance in their own preaching?

When seeking to improve our preaching, the tendency is to focus on mechanics. This very rarely proves helpful. It certainly does not go far enough. Various techniques may resolve quirks in our delivery, but they will not bring forth the honest dynamic most of us desire. There's only so much someone can tell us *not* to do. Those things which really improve delivery have little to do with mechanics. They have to do with the heart, soul and mind of the preacher.

Some of our favorite preachers have very poor mechanics according to textbook standards. The most engaging preachers often have the greatest number of mechanical quirks. Yet, those quirks make sense. Their delivery is more a manifestation of who they are as individuals and followers of Christ. What we are witnessing is the impact of sincere discovery in their lives. This realization lies at the core of this book. Fundamentally, it does not really matter what (or who) you "sound like" as long as (you're biblical and) you sound like you should.

For those who can relate, the logic surrounding the three characteristics (*clarity*, *simplicity* and *passion*) is a little bit of *Karate Kid*: "Wax on! Wax off!" I've chosen to focus on those matters which precede and lie beneath techniques. As in everything we do, those things which truly please God begin with sincerity in the inner man. Clarity, simplicity and passion are intrinsic qualities, not mechanical. Concentrating on internal realities will naturally improve your delivery. More to the point, it will set your delivery free.

Clarity is the starting point for dynamic delivery, not rehearsal and structure. A Spirit-illumined understanding and clarity of the text liberates delivery by allowing it to depend upon conviction and not structure. Structure, which is essential, results from and serves clarity. The best example of this is Dr. John F. MacArthur.

Clarity leads to *simplicity*. Understanding a text or biblical concept on an intimate level affords us the opportunity to present difficult concepts to a wide range of intellects and apply it to unlimited context. But depth of understanding is only helpful so far as we are able to explain it in simple and universally comprehensible ways. This is the exact area in which most expositors struggle. We're hard to understand. How well you understand something is measured by how well you can explain it to others. It's all about simplification. What we need is "understandability." The best example of this principle is Dr. R.C. Sproul.

Finally, we come to *passion*—a rather elusive quality for expositors. Transitioning from the scholarship required to understand a truth to a disposition concomitant with that truth is difficult for most of us. "Feel" is not a word we're comfortable using to describe our aims as preachers. But we should not allow various abuses of it to dissuade us from passion's importance. Rather, we should reclaim it from those who have made a mockery of it. Passion—defined herein—is the manifestation of sincere conviction through the transparent expression of the preacher in the preaching moment. Dr. John Piper is the logical choice here.

Here it is in one shot. *Clarity,* which intensifies the impact of truth in our hearts and minds, leads to *simplicity. Simplicity* creates a comprehensive awareness of truth which results in a sincere *passion. Passion* allows us to communicate truth with a biblically authoritative impact. A preacher naturally moves from one to the other—from clarity to simplicity to passion. There's a specific sequence here; one cannot precede another or exist without the other. I cannot be endowed with a sincere passion unless there is a depth of understanding. Depth of understanding comes with clarity. Clarity comes with hard work and grace.

Ultimately, all this points to one substantial reality. The big secret behind the most dynamic and admirable expositors we know is obvious: *There is no big secret.* It comes down to what it always comes down to—a simple and undefiled devotion to our glorious God, an earnest love for the eternal Son and a constant dependence on the Holy Spirit to do what He alone can do.

Assumptions: Some Broader Aims of this Book

In addition to verifying my core argument, there were other goals I set for myself. I wanted to test the general assumptions about expository preaching I had carried around my entire ministry. I wanted to test them against some of the most respected opinions on the subject. Many of these assumptions had become deep-seated obstacles in my exposition and delivery. I was reevaluating core convictions surrounding the relationship between expository preaching and delivery. It was here I faced the elephant.

I was surprised to discover how many preachers that I admire disagreed with or minimized some of the basic presuppositions I was operating under. In the end, what I believed was true and widely assumed by the finest expositors wasn't. This particular experience was life transforming.

I was also surprised by how many of these same men were frustrated by the pervasive stereotype(s) of expository preaching. Most of them believe it suffers from a misrepresentation brought on by well-meaning, but imbalanced practitioners. Nearly all those I interacted with pushed back against some label in one way or another.

Somewhere along the way I also realized my struggle was part of a wider trend. I was part of a simultaneous re-commitment and re-examination of expository preaching underway by my generation of expositors. While rejecting the extremes of pragmatic seeker methodologies, recycled social gospel emergent trends and the rancorous remains of hardened fundamentalism, there was a need to get one's bearings in the *post-everything* context in which we were preaching.[2] The greater purpose was the same. The human condition was the same. The message was the same. But much had changed about the variables between our proclamation of the truth and the front pew. It was the same old enemy with modern weaponry. Every generation of expositors is forced to wrestle with questions surrounding their context. As it turns out, there are a lot of preachers asking these same questions.

Qualifications: How to Approach This Book

My aim in this work is not to recapture surrendered ground. That is, I take certain theological and methodological convictions for granted.

---

2   Kevin DeYoung and Ted Kluck, *Why We're Not Emergent: By Two Guys Who Should Be* (Moody: Chicago, 2008); David W. Henderson, *Culture Shift: Communicating God's Truth to Our Changing World* (Baker: Grand Rapids, 1998).

My audience is comprised of men who live and breathe the biblical axioms I hold. These truths bind us together. Ours is a specific fraternity. I'm not "preaching about the need for preaching." I'm writing *to* expositors about practical issues of delivery. I'm calling us back from the ledge of academic obscurantism.

Furthermore, I'm not writing to convince others about the priority of exposition. There is an abundance of work on this subject. Mine is an intramural discussion. As a result, I spend very little time arguing for the authority of God's Word or the merit of expository preaching as compared to some other model. I assume both. I do not offer an extensive definition of what constitutes expository preaching. I present a brief one and then assume we know what's entailed.

Furthermore, I don't go out of my way to present a biblical/theological qualifier for every suggestion or exhortation I offer toward some practical or philosophical adjustment. In this sense, this is not an *exposition* about *exposition*. For instance, if I suggest "real power in delivery is found in passion" I don't mean this in any exclusive way. Obviously, the real power comes from the Holy Spirit. I only mean to emphasize the importance of this particular element of delivery. The reader will need to cede me the benefit of the doubt in various places. However, in order to reassure you, I offer the following quote from a later chapter,

> We (I) believe the Bible is divine in its origin. We (I) believe this, therefore, we (I) also believe the Bible to be true, literal, infallible and without error. We (I) also believe it should be accurately explained. Furthermore, we (I) believe the Spirit's power alone can translate it and transform lives by it. Additionally, we (I) firmly believe our responsibility is to present it without distortion.

I also assume that most expositors struggle with delivery. Therefore, I have a tendency to generalize. My generalizations are based on a combination of personal experience, research, observation and journalism. What I present as a "flaw" in our delivery is somewhat of a dirty little secret among our fraternity. If you're the exception, please accept my apology. But nearly every preacher I spoke with—whether officially, or unofficially—readily acknowledged the dull edge for which exposition is often known. It frustrates them. Additionally, they were all quick to agree with the assessment that expositors, generally speaking, are the least dynamic and struggle more in the area of delivery than any other preachers.

Descriptions like "human tranquilizers," "running commentaries" and "angry prophets" that I employ herein were borrowed from my discussions with your favorite preachers. If you are offended by some of my characterizations, chances are they hit their intended mark. But, at the same time, my intent is not to condemn the majority of expositors as poor craftsmen. Quite the contrary, I believe most *are* tremendous craftsmen who need to be liberated from some faulty assumptions about biblical preaching.

Encouragements: The Aim of This Book

The ten feet from the front pew to the pulpit are the most significant any preacher travels in a given week. It's hard for an observer to fully appreciate the strange combination of agony and delight joining forces to make that walk possible. There's no such thing as an average sermon. For any faithful expositor, the distance is paved with blood, sweat and tears. Those few sheets of paper resting in the back of our Bibles are everything. We step up every week hoping a little of our life-changing encounter with the Word of God gets through. This expectation fills our very soul.

Every preacher knows the disappointment of unmet expectations. We've all descended from the pulpit having delivered a "dog." The ten feet out is now fifty back. It's a long lonely journey to our seat. Some of our sermons are better than we think. And then ... some are worse than we imagine. No matter how severely our gracious victims have suffered, none suffers more than the preacher. The pain is not just over poor delivery. It's what our poor delivery did. It got in-between God and His people.

We have treasures on the tip of our tongue and can't get them out. We know what we want to say. We just can't find the words when it matters most. Sometimes we do and it all comes together. Those are sublime moments. Unfortunately, they're also rare. But, do they have to be? Is consistency possible? Can we expect to consistently deliver the discoveries of our study without losing their intended impact? I think so. In fact, I've seen it done. I've listened to preachers my entire

Christian life whose legacy is the consistent delivery of powerful sermons. This reliability is admirable. It also raises significant questions. How have they done it? Is this merely gifting? (Yes and no.) Can it be learned? (Yes and no.) How did they find their voice? Most importantly, can their constancy be emulated? What makes them powerful preachers? I had the amazing fortune of sitting down—face to face—with some incredibly gifted and humble expositors. I let them speak for themselves. In the moments they gave me, I mined them for every little insight I could get. It was self-serving joy.

Ambitions: The Hope of This Book

My aim is to inspire. To inspire expositors to go forth and wake the slumbering Church by setting themselves and their exegesis on fire behind the pulpit. To view the preaching moment and their delivery as a glorious and recurring opportunity to exalt Christ through the "foolish" act of biblically-based proclamation. To be unashamed fools and workmen for Christ. To preach with an enviable blindness most will never experience over the course of their entire lives. A blindness to the "fickle faces" of people.

This book is intended to be an "easy read," not a comprehensive tome on preaching. It's far from it. It would be best if you started it on Monday with a view toward Sunday. It will take little time to work through. Chances are you'll set it down halfway through in order to apply something these gifted men suggest. That would be even better. In fact, that's perfect. All the men I interviewed walked away from the dialogue refreshed and enthused about preaching. If you come away excited about the privilege of preaching, I've achieved my goal. I pray it will be a blessing to you as well. I pray you find a new passion to conquer those ten feet this Sunday. I pray for "well-driven nails."

Swing hard!

Chapter One

Authenticity and the Freedom of Finding Your Voice

You know as a businessman, I've been in rotary for almost forty years, and every month we have a meeting and someone gives a talk of some sort. When I go home, I can tell my wife what the talk was about, and how the person made his point. I can rarely do that with sermons. I think we should shut the theological seminaries down and send our candidates to Rotary International.[3]

Death by Power Point

For many the prospect of listening to expository (biblical) preaching is equivalent to a business meeting with one of those painfully bad power point presentations complete with stock transitions where slides are read line for line. An effect known as "death by power point." In the course of an hour (if you're lucky) facts are delivered, but no one remembers them or why they are worth remembering. Expository preaching has a bad reputation among many for being dull and irrelevant. In defense we offer more dignified descriptive alternatives like "serious" and "biblical." But there is some truth to the stereotype. We who laud it most have

---

3   David T. Gordon, *Why Johnny Can't Preach: The Media Have Shaped the Messages* (P&R: Philipsburg, New Jersey, 2009), p. 21.

done it no favors by confirming the suspicion through lackluster pulpits. Obviously, it's not true in every case, but practitioners of the craft too often "say something" without having had "something to say." As one well-known expositor noted, "Thorough exegesis and clear organization are crucial to an effective message. But a good sermon poorly preached is no better than a poor sermon properly preached."[4]

While visiting a good friend—an avid listener of sermons and a sober-minded believer—the topic of exposition came up. It was raised out of frustration. "I prefer topical preaching over expository. It applies more to my life." Her criticism is somewhat standard. It's also at the core of my frustration. For one, the contrast drawn with topical preaching demonstrates a fundamental misunderstanding of what constitutes expository preaching. While it usually is (and should be) consecutive in nature, it does not exclude topical or thematic presentations. It only means the topics or themes are founded on the sound exegesis of passages in their original context and not the musing of some pastor plucking passages out of mid-air.

This generalization was bothersome enough, but my friend completed the stereotype by dropping the A word—*application.* How many times have we heard that? "Expository preaching lacks relevance and application." On the contrary expository preaching is the most *applicational* of all methodologies! At least it should be. (A point I will stress below.)

All this was streaming through my head as I formulated a response to my friend's sweeping criticism. Rather than overwhelm her with a diatribe (or lose a friendship), I said simply, "Obviously, you've never actually heard expository preaching. At least, as it's meant to be." Sadly, most haven't.

My beef is not with the method itself. For the record, I view exposition as the only legitimate form of preaching. I completely reject the modern criticisms of traditional preaching.[5] Explaining the Bible is preaching. Exposition by definition means to explain or expose. It

---

4   John MacArthur Jr. et al., *Rediscovering Expository Preaching: Balancing the Science and Art of Biblical Exposition* (Word: Dallas, 1992), p. 321.

5   Doug Paggit, *Preaching Re-imagined: The Role of the Sermon in Communities of Faith* (Zondervan: Grand Rapids, 2005).

includes both the process of uncovering the Bible's intended meaning in its original context and the responsibility to present that meaning to God's people who sit in a different context. This is the very gap that exposition seeks to bridge.[6] When the preacher is finished, God's people understand better what God has said in His Word.

Such is the distinguishing feature of expository preaching. It carries with it certain implications. Sermons may not be expository or biblical simply because the Bible is referenced. In the same way that standing in a garage does not make one a car, standing behind a pulpit with a Bible does not make one an expositor. There are plenty of congregants who hear "preachy" and assume their pastor is biblical. Just because it sounds like "traditional" preaching does not mean that it's biblical preaching. Biblical preaching has a distinct resonance. You know it when you hear it.

Piles of Bricks and Lumber Everywhere

My homiletics courses were scheduled in my last year of seminary. I gained innumerable helpful insights about preaching. In many ways it was time well spent. But I've also spent some time—two decades—unlearning some bad habits which have proven to be a hindrance to my mindset in delivery.

Deriving my sermons and sermon structure from exegesis was the primary focus of my homiletics. This is as it should be. My education, for which I am eternally grateful, left me with a working knowledge of the biblical languages. I'm now aware of their nuance and am able to recognize and work through the majority of interpretive issues. I start with an open Greek (or Hebrew) Bible every week. Furthermore, I'm able to interact with commentaries written by men who actually know what they're doing. In this I am adequately equipped.

There is a part of me, however, which has struggled to overcome the resulting—and unintentional—imbalance. Unfortunately, I approached any instruction on delivery as a footnote on the primary emphasis of hermeneutics and exegesis. I failed to integrate it into my thinking as an extension of exegesis. As a result, in my departure from seminary I struggled to take all the incredible information exegesis

---

6   Roy B. Zuck, *Basic Bible Interpretation: A Practical Guide to Discovering Biblical Truth* (Victor: Colorado Springs, 1991), p. 16.

yields and present it in an impactful way. I did my exegesis no favors by marginalizing delivery.

The sermons I developed (and continued to develop for some time) were basically very succinct, reasonably structured and occasionally interesting information dumps. My operational assumption? Technical equals biblical. For certain, my homiletic was a safeguard against the pragmatic abuses of the seeker movement, but not much else. Any consideration of how a concept should be presented or any creative approach to presentation was suspect. I was obtaining my structures from exegesis but agonizing in my presentation (as was my audience.) Ultimately, my sermons—and study for that matter—were perpetually unfinished. As Broadus put it, "Piles of bricks and lumber and sand are as much a house as the mere piling up of thoughts will constitute a discourse."[7]

I had "piles of bricks and lumber." I had gathered the facts but had no idea how to process and present them. Basically, I could not finish. More importantly, I could not bridge the gap between my study and the hearts of my people—which is at the core of the expository method.

> *Nothing could be more frustrating and discouraging to the interpreter than to have a message fall flat and lifeless on an audience after the interpreter has met all the requirements of investigating grammar, syntax, literary structure, and history of a given text. After the exegete has invested all those hours conscientiously translating the text, parsing the verbs, investigating the historical backgrounds, and tracing the syntactical relationships, there is a feeling of betrayal when all that labor fails to deliver a credible message that will speak to modern men and women.*[8]

I was committed to studying fifteen to twenty hours per week, but very little of that time was spent considering "how to say it." What I ended up doing, rather than preaching, was inadvertently taking my audience through a weekly Basic Bible Interpretation class from the pulpit. I was "Master of the Obvious!"

---

7   John A. Broadus, *On the Preparation and Delivery of Sermons*, 4th ed., Revised by Vernon Stanfield, (Harper Collins, New York, 1979), p.225.

8   Walter C. Kaiser, *Toward an Exegetical Theology: Biblical Exegesis for Preaching and Teaching* (Baker: Grand Rapids, 1981), p. 131.

Preaching labs, which are designed to treat issues of delivery, bear a striking resemblance to oncology. The treatment for cancer is nearly as lethal as the condition. In the same way, the treatment for bad preaching is just as lethal as the condition. Namely, listening. Listening to bad sermons is barely survivable. None suffer more than the audience. The most lethal are found in seminary preaching labs. Preaching labs are a relentless barrage of really predictable, really dreadful sermons. It's like watching the first few weeks of *American Idol* when we constantly wonder: "Who told this person he could sing? Or "Can't she hear herself?" It's painful to watch.

While suffering through these sermons (including mine), I was struck by an observation: "They all sound the same." They had the same mechanical ting of the "three of this" and "four of that" format. But I wondered: *Is this really the desired result of the historical grammatical method?* It all seemed forced upon the text and the preacher. We were "clones" was my thought. Mere copies of what we assumed constituted an expository delivery. It all raised important questions in my mind: *Was this the only way to approach biblical preaching? Is this what exposition should sound like?*

> It's like watching the first few weeks of American Idol when we constantly wonder: "Who told this person he could sing?

Eventually, I fell upon an important personal discovery. There is no direct connection between a particular style of delivery and expository preaching. Not one that could be defended biblically. In reality, every method of delivery is capable of obscuring the meaning of the text, including a very structured one. Like many of the ones I heard in those labs. Steve Smith, associate professor of preaching at Southwestern Seminary, explained it this way,

> I do not believe that the expository style should be understood as the only way to preach because exposition is not a style per se. It may seem like splitting hairs, but think about it. If the person means a specific stylized sermonic structure (i.e., three or four points, an introduction and a conclusion), then I could not defend that structural style as the only way to go. This is not because I do not have a high view of Scripture; rather this is precisely because

> *I have too high a view of Scripture to take the precious Word of*
> *God, with its multiple genres that God inspired to communicate*
> *Himself, and force it to fit a predetermined outline.*[9]

He's right. After all, if Paul wanted to share "Ten Foundations of Christian Living" why didn't he just say that? What I saw was rather artificial. Where was the intended impact of the passage? Where was the heart and soul of the preacher? Where was the evidence of spirit-illumined clarity in the preacher's life?

I'm not opposed to structured delivery. It's unavoidable since there is an order in the text. Furthermore, our people need structure. It gives them a hook to hang their mind on. Additionally, our professors required a certain format for a reason. As young preachers we needed training wheels. But—and here is the problem—no one ever explained how to take them off.

Getting Over the Hump

After years of practice, certain aspects of preaching are just as hard as they've ever been. In some ways they're harder. Not necessarily the more mechanical aspects. Time, practice and tools have helped expedite some components of preparation. What's remained relentlessly painful is the end of the process. I still find myself on my knees beseeching the mercy of God at the same place in the process every week. It's that moment I turn from the details and face the blank canvas of my sermon. Getting my heart down there is hard work. Humanly speaking, it's what we do in this place as expositors that makes the greatest difference in our preaching. It's here the real sermon is forged and the real preacher comes to life. Obviously, we start with the original language, but getting to the common language is always hardest. It's the blood sweat and tears of the process.

As I traveled the country interviewing preachers, I came to realize something—we all grind at the same spot. It's the same for every conscientious biblical preacher. No matter how experienced or gifted, we face the same difficult question every week, "How am I going to

---

9   Steve Smith, *Dying to Preach: Embracing the Cross and the Pulpit* (Kregel: Grand Rapids, 2009), p. 64.

say this?" Not one of the gifted men I spoke with ever mentioned having prayed to understand a verb tense. But they've all prayed for the ability to prove the importance of that verb tense to their people.

Making our way from exegesis to the pulpit and then into our people's hearts is exhausting. Fact is, after you take the passage apart through exegesis—thoroughly examining every feature and are comfortable you understand it and how it fits within the larger context—your preparation has just begun. As Martyn Lloyd-Jones said:

> Though the sermon has been prepared in the way we have indicated, and prepared carefully, yet the preacher must be free in the act of preaching, in the delivery of the sermon. He must not be too tied to his preparation and by it. This is a crucial point: this is of the very essence of this act of preaching.[10]

Many expositors have no idea how to get over the proverbial hump of delivery. Maybe it's because no one ever showed us how. We're banging it out the hard way. Others of us, paralyzed by false assumptions, can't bring ourselves to try. We've inherited a suspicion of anything remotely different. We reject anything which does not fit a familiar format. Having witnessed the abuses of church growth gurus, we consider anything other than a particular structure a major compromise.

There is a lot of "creative" preaching out there worthy of rejection. Specifically, a type of preaching more dependent upon the quality of lighting and Christianized *feng shui* than exegesis. Its message and application has little to do with the passages on which it is based. It's the kind of stuff you could get from a self-help seminar down at the YMCA. I call it "Soccer Mom Theology" or "Free Group Therapy." This is not what I'm advocating.

No matter the particular manner of delivery, style or format, expository preaching will always be evidenced by certain characteristics. Expository preaching transcends delivery. At its core it will always be an explanation of what the Bible means, and any application will result from that intended meaning. But this does not necessitate a certain style. It only necessitates a certain conviction.

---

10   D. Martyn Lloyd-Jones, *Preaching and Preachers* (Zondervan: Grand Rapids, 1971), p. 83.

That Long Intimidating Shadow

Hundreds of books are written on preaching every year. The obvious question? Why another one? What else could possibly be said on this subject that has not already been said? I've considered this plenty of times. I realize men with much more practical experience and more substantial credentials have written on the subject. Legends of exposition, who many want to hear from, have weighed in on preaching. There are classics which cast vast shadows on any modern treatment, even the good ones. Furthermore, I've chosen to write at a time when preaching has fallen out of favor in the Church.[11] Quite frankly, interest is low. I also admit that my knowledge is limited. I write more from a hacker's point of view than a pro's. I'm no professor of homiletics. So why listen to me?

If this project were strictly about homiletics, I would have stopped a long time ago. But it's not about preaching per se. It's about the preacher's heart. It's about a journey every preacher needs to make. One that ends in the liberation of a preacher's voice. In all my research and interviews, it became evident that the majority of truly effective preachers had taken their own journey at some moment in their ministries. A journey which ended for each of them in the freedom of his pulpit, the liberation of his exegesis and the discovery of his voice.

On a practical level, every effective preacher is effective primarily because he has found his *voice*. Whether he realizes it or not, every frustrated preacher is searching for his. Obviously, some things only time and practice can correct. The ups and downs of regular delivery are part of the process. But every preacher whom we admire shares a similar story repeated in various ways. They all began with the same frustration: "I have to find my style of preaching." If we intend to do our exegesis any favors, we have to get to the same place. As it is, there are two substantial challenges standing between us and this enviable freedom we hear in their preaching—transparency and fear.

---

11   Steve Lawson, *Famine in the Land: A Passionate Call for Expository Preaching* (Moody: Chicago, 2003).

Transparency: Taking the Plastic off Our Pulpits

My inspiration to write has been based on an assumption: I'm a thirty-something young, reformed pastor-teacher desperate to preach with a God-glorifying sincerity, *and* there must be at least one other preacher out there who shares my desperation *and* is processing through the same challenges.

This man inspires me. I'm writing especially to him. He's my comrade making his way through the same iterations in his own life. He's the pastor out there in the trenches comfortable knowing his fame will probably never reach beyond his name's inclusion in Sunday's bulletin. The preacher who few know and few ever will; he's a plodder. A servant who cranks out one "average" sermon after another week after week. He's a conscientious expositor who agonizes over the details of the text long before he ascends the pulpit. He's caught somewhere between the fundamentalism of his father and the latest "church-in-a-box" craze delivered to his door. With innumerable other responsibilities on his plate, he answers the bell tolling for his sermon every week. He has preached with real freedom a few times in his life but wants to every Sunday. He has no time to reinvent his homiletics, but he knows they could greatly improve. I sat down and wrote to and for that guy. Why him? Because that's me. He and I, despite never having met, share a common struggle. My message is aimed at him.

Here's the connection to the delivery of sermons. I'm motivated by a similar perspective when I preach. There has to be at least one sinner out there who can relate to my own moment of clarity in this passage. I preach to people like me who face the daily struggle against sin and depend moment by moment upon the grace of God. This axiom hovers above my preparation and emerges in my preaching. By grace I'm compelled to understand God's Word and communicate it in a manner that will help translate it and apply it in the lives of those I love. This takes transparency.

"Your people will not care what you *know* until they *know* you care." I've heard this proverb a thousand times. There's a lot of truth in it. Sincerity is indispensably important. But the type of sincerity which communicates best goes a little beyond this. God's people not only need to know you care; they also need to know that what you've come to believe has changed your life. I'm not only called to explain the truth, but to exemplify it (1 Timothy 4:12). This includes the weekly, daily, moment-by-moment impact of the truth on my life. Effectiveness in preaching is tied to the preacher's own pursuit of God. Our people need to observe us stunned by the truths we encounter. Do not underestimate the power of an "unveiled face" in the preaching moment. Among the most hopeful, powerful, effective things I can do for my people is to drag a freshly broken heart into the pulpit.

Hiding Behind Suits and Syntax

Not long ago I was invited to preach out of state. I delivered a sermon in which I used my own life as an example of the struggle. Even as a pastor, I face a constant battle to remain consistent in the spiritual leadership of my family. I shared a particular challenge I had faced in this regard. It was a rather light-hearted moment of self-effacement. An anecdote. I gave it little consideration at the time—my own congregation would think nothing of it—but my transparency had a major impact on the church I was visiting. In fact, it may have communicated the text more effectively than any particular thing I said.

Afterwards while talking with one of the elders, a church member made this observation, "When Byron offered his example, I was taken aback. It occurred to me that he too is a sinner and struggles against sin like I do. It was a relief to see grace at work in him. It gave me hope as a father and husband." Referencing his own pastor he continued, "I think our pastor struggles with sin. But for the life of me, I've never heard him mention it. I've often wondered if he's human like I'm human."

While I did not intend this comparison and greatly admire that pastor, I was thankful the church member noticed my transparency because it was intentional. I was trying to be a tangible example of sanctifying grace. This type of vulnerable clarity has a way of turning the theological *textbooks* in our people's minds into *hymnbooks* in their hearts. We cannot be aloof and untouchable. We cannot hide our humanity behind suits or syntax.

Many pastors would argue this type of transparency diminishes the authority of the pulpit and reduces people's confidence in our ministry. Consequently, they hold their humanity back. They consider it part of their responsibility to keep personal foibles out of view. The result, in my humble opinion, is a starched oratory, not sermons delivered by human instruments. If expository preaching has a bad reputation as boring and lifeless, it's partly a result of this mindset. There's a lot wrong with this perspective. Its greatest failure is the distance it puts between our pulpits and the front row. It's a distance most of us struggle to bridge every week in delivery. We're too often "expository scientists." We apply the proper investigative methods to the text resulting in sound conclusions. Our preaching discloses the results of our investigation, but rarely why it's important. "Next slide please!"

Expository preaching does not have to be mechanical and sterile to pass as legitimate. It would seem a grammatical historical method should result in a more dynamic delivery. After all, the expositor spends the majority of his week crushing his heart under the authorial intent of the passage. There's no way we truly prepare to preach and then walk away from our studies unchanged. If we do, we have not yet begun to prepare and are certainly not prepared to preach. Whatever the Word intends to effect in us—brokenness, passion, conviction, righteous indignation, contrition, clarity, joy, exultation, hope, zeal—it must come through in our delivery. We must expose our people to the Word's effect in our own heart. How can we not? It is the natural overflow of the expositional approach.

> There's no way we truly prepare to preach and then walk away from our studies unchanged. If we do, we have not yet begun to prepare and are certainly not prepared to preach.

Because we are called to pursue and exemplify godliness, there must be discretion in our transparency and in what we present as examples from our own lives. But such openness does not result in a lack of respect from our people. It results in the exact opposite—trust. The demonstration of God's grace in our own lives—transparency—enhances our authority. It instills confidence in our ministry; it does not erode it. It makes us examples of what His power looks like in a life. It endears our people to us as shepherds and gives us their ear as preachers. It puts the Gospel on display through our own experience. "Wearing plastic" in the pulpit has a way of keeping the cross in the realm of the theoretical. All this changes when we take that plastic off.

The Bible itself proves this point. It contains a refreshingly candid description of God's servants. Their flaws are an obvious and important part of their repertoire. In certain places in the Bible, the humanity is raw, and there was no effort to filter it out. God's servants are certainly not the marble statues we've made them out to be. Their failures echo in their exhortations. Or should we assume Peter's encouragement to remain faithful to Christ (1 Peter 4:12-14) wasn't offered in light of his own historic failure?

Or do we think Paul's passionate explanation of an alien righteousness (Philippians 3:7-11) was not delivered within view of his own pathetic self-righteous dung heap? Paul said of himself and his own ministry,

> *It is a trustworthy statement, deserving full acceptance, that Christ Jesus came into the world to save sinners, among whom I am foremost of all. And yet for this reason I found mercy, in order that in me as the foremost, Jesus Christ might demonstrate His perfect patience, as an example for those who would believe in Him for eternal life. (1 Timothy 1:15-16)*

Being "above reproach" is not the same as being above our people. Fact is we're down there with them at the foot of the cross even when we're up there in the pulpit. We have to aim our exegesis, delivery and heart at these precious people.

Real Life, Real People, Real Absurd

This discussion is not about relevance. Relevance is a trap preachers are forced into by epidemic demands for *over-principalized* teaching. In my estimation, placing too much emphasis on one's ability to be relevant results in a peculiar bondage. As one notable scholar pointed out, "Relevance is relative… The preacher needs to beware. A lot of congratulations and noise about relevance and how the Lord blessed us through the sermon or talk can be very seductive. Relevance can be easily assessed on purely pragmatic grounds."[12] If we give into the demand for relevance, we end up sounding more like life coaches

---

12   Graeme Goldsworthy, *Preaching the Whole Bible as Christian Scripture: The Application of Biblical Theology to Expository Preaching* (Eerdmans, Grand Rapids, 2000), p. 61.

than heralds of divine truth. Paul warned that to do so was to give away the Gospel (1 Corinthians 1:17).

As it is, relevance and "just add water "applications are upheld by evangelicals as the most desirable virtues a preacher can posses. Various clichés which facilitate this shortsightedness are everywhere: "Just give me what I can use.""Where's the application to my life?""I want preaching where the rubber meets the road." "Real life, real people, real issues." Are we serious? Despite what we may think, there's no virtue underlying these statements. We assume they represent some more noble commitment to spiritual things. In reality, this mindset could not be more self-absorbed and contrary to biblical spirituality.

After I preached a theological sermon on a particular attribute of God, a rather self-confident matriarch approached me. I knew what was coming. You always know what's coming. It *ain't* good. "There was nothing in that sermon which hit me. It had no application to my life."

Basically, "you're not good at preaching." In her own way, she was trying to be helpful. She's what Warren Wiersbe calls a "well-intentioned dragon." Unfortunately, she picked the wrong moment.

As I had been preaching, I noticed a gracious elderly woman in our congregation who had recently been widowed. Her husband died of a heart attack while climbing into bed one evening. She attempted CPR, but he was gone. He was a godly man; she was a loving wife. They were one flesh for more than fifty years. During the sermon, she wept. Eyes closed with a contented smile on her face. Let's just say the sermon applied. When my self-appointed homiletics professor finished her critique, I drew her attention to the tear-stained cheeks of the precious woman. Motionless. Still absorbed in the greatness of God. No explanation was necessary. But, of course, I explained it to her anyway. Due to our obsession with "relevance," our contemporary mindset fails to consider the heart in the pew next to us. All we seem to care about any more are happier marriages, better sex and personal contentment. It's mind-numbing narcissism.

The pressure put on the preacher to be "relevant" is intense. It can overwhelm you. Many end up compromising in the wrong direction. Before you change your wardrobe or adjust the lighting in your sanctuary, I offer this alternative for both preacher and parishioner—*heartfelt transparency.*

As a preacher, I stand before fellow sinners saved by grace through faith. Their sinful condition is as obvious to them as mine is to me. They realize, as I do, the need for divine remedies and not empty suggestions. Together we stand before an open Bible, knowing the Word of God is living and active and the only source of Truth. We also confess the Holy Spirit as the only real agent of change. Prior to the invasion of Grace in our lives, our own wisdom led us to despair. We spent our lives bowing at the altar of relevance. Then a gracious God opened our eyes and saved our souls. When He did, we abandoned our so-called wisdom and repented of our self-absorption.

By its very nature, preaching is ignoring man's opinion. We have been called to speak on behalf of God. Let God speak. Let man listen. Why not allow the Word of God to crush and rebuild me and then carry that transforming message to those people I love who are yearning for the same thing? That's real. That seems relevant.

Preach the Word. This is the only alternative to all the clamoring for relevance and the resulting nonsense that passes for preaching in too many churches. There's no need for all that "stuff." I've lost count of the "new" approaches. I can't keep up. Why not preach with transparency? Why not understand it and let it transform you? Carry that burden to the pulpit and allow it to transform others. The more you understand it, the more it transforms everyone. This simple aim transcends styles, methods of delivery, personality, education, etc. Herein is freedom. Freedom from expectations. Freedom from the limitations of our giftedness. Freedom to preach with authority and passion. Freedom from the fear of men.

Fearlessness: Blind to Be an Instrument

The fear of man is brutal. It's a beast. It's that lump in your throat when you hear someone is leaving your church or a member calls a meeting with one of those infamous one point agendas: "I just need to talk to you about some concerns." Fear is paralyzing at times. It's also sin. Whether you realize it or not, fear of men is also your greatest challenge in the act of preaching. It's a force to be reckoned with. If we are ever going to truly preach, we have to face it head on.

We preachers are an insecure breed. Who else goes fishing for compliments as often as we do? Our happiness is too often tied to the faces of fickle people. It's possible to spend most of our ministry preaching for the approval of some unseen group or living in the shadow of unrealistic comparisons. All this is man-pleasing at its best. Our confidence as biblical communicators thrives when we are liberated from this burden. A preacher rightly said, "…when you are free from your people's smiles and frowns, you are at liberty to be an instrument of blessing to them. I submit that if there is to be increased power in the pulpit, there must be a return to the purity of motivation comprised of a fear of God."[13]

There are plenty of respectable opinions to which we could cater. There's that group of people who judge our preaching based on its immediate connection to their lives. There's that other group with lexicons and Greek texts in hand waiting to assist us in our grammar. And then there are those who tell us how well we do every Sunday—whether it's true or not.

What must grip us above all else is a concern for God and the task He's given us. It must overshadow every other consideration, including any concern for our limitations or inability. We must declare what God has said regardless of which group of people stand before us. Ironically, in order to do that, we must preach with a sanctified disregard for their opinions. It's a courageous love. There's David who faced the giant. Then there's the prophet Nathan who faced the giant-killer. Which took more courage?

We can't spend our time concerning ourselves with what others think of us or our skill-sets. We must be blind to all men, especially ourselves. The most important person to ignore is you; an unhealthy level of self-consciousness can be more intimidating than a congregation full of critics.

Don't take my admonition as a license for rebellion. We must remain humble, receiving even the harshest criticism with grace. Some arrogant preachers set themselves above the counsel of others in order to justify shoddy hermeneutics or inadequate preparation. Such

---

13 A.N. Martin, *What's Wrong with Preaching Today?* (Banner of Truth: Carlisle, PA, 1967), p. 17-18.

is foolish insecurity. There is always room for improvement. But you will die a slow, agonizing death behind the pulpit and in ministry if you seek to satisfy people's fancies or try to emulate someone's style.

To do so is contrary to the very act preaching. When Paul charged Timothy he did not say, "I charge you in the presence of your congregation!" Nor did he say, "I charge you in the presence of your seminary professors!" He charged Timothy in the "presence of God and Christ Jesus who is to judge the living and the dead." As often as we reference this text, you would think we'd take the command seriously. At some point we have to put the opinions of men aside and preach what we know with the gifts we have in the presence of God. Otherwise, all we have is a more respectable idolatry.

> *Preachers that fear men are more concerned about what people think about their preaching than what God thinks about their preaching. They are more concerned about failing human expectations for their preaching than failing the Holy Spirit's expectations for their preaching.* [14]

It's Hard to Preach with Your Hands around Your Throat

For years my preaching felt awkward. It was like being forty and trying to wear a suit which fit when I was twenty. Over the years, unknowingly, I had grown out of it. Coming of age in ministry is normal. It happens to everyone. I had changed as a preacher and as a pastor. What once fit was now restrictive. When I look back, I see it clearly. I was a caricature of what I had been told a preacher should be. I was faithful to the text, but I was not free to preach. It was like the frustration one feels when preaching through a translator; when the depth of your passion is lost in translation. It's unnatural and difficult.

Due to my fundamentalist background, my fall-back position was always torching some straw man. I was too often the "angry prophet." But this was not consistent with who I was out of the pulpit. Generally speaking, I'm a people person and a shepherd at heart. I love to mix it up with the congregation on all kinds of levels. The Church is my life and the people I face every Sunday are my dearest friends.

---

14   Greg Heilser, *Spirit Led Preaching: The Holy Spirit's Role in Sermon Preparation and Delivery* (B&H: Nashville, 2007), p. 148.

Our rapport is a great gift from God. But there was a disconnect between my on-the-ground experience and my experience in the pulpit. Don't misunderstand! There is a time and place for a tone of warning. It's a critical part of defending the truth and protecting the sheep. Consecutive exposition leads to these types of messages and emphases. I definitely have that gear. But not every passage has that tone and stress. Depending on the passage, a preacher may be required to weep, rejoice, laugh or repent. It's the nature of exposition. But I, on the other hand, was a one-hit wonder.

Coming of age was extremely frustrating, but I did come to understand the problem. I was trying to be someone else. More specifically, I was trying to please someone else. If I was ever really going to preach, I had to become comfortable in my own skin. When I did, all the baggage fell away. When this happened, my people noticed. My wife noticed. I noticed. It was my liberation. One preacher accurately captured the essence of this transformation,

> *The most important aspect of a preacher's style is authenticity. When I started preaching, I thought my 'style' had to fit a certain category. As a result I mimicked some of my favorite preachers. I was constantly reinventing myself. Ultimately, I had to find my own 'style' and stick with it. That meant there was one less thing I had to manufacture. I had to realize that God gave me a unique personality and he intended to use it in unique ways.*[15]

I now know exactly what he means. Coming to understand it for myself was a long and exacerbating walk.

Some specific experiences led to my own freedom. Experience has a way of teaching what theory cannot. The most dramatic came when I was invited to preach a chapel service at my *alma mater*. A huge privilege. Naturally, I wanted to do a good job for my professors. As I looked around the chapel, the men on the first three rows were some of the smartest on the planet. Those in the remaining fifteen rows thought they were. A *slightly* daunting venue! And the

---

15   Voddie Baucham, "Ten Questions for Expositors," Unashamed Workman, http://www.unashamedworkman.wordpress.com/2007/04/18/10-questions-for-expositors-voddie-baucham (accessed February 2009).

result? In short, it was a disaster. Let's just say that it's hard to preach with your hands around your throat. When I stood up, all I could see were grades and evaluations staring back at me. The pressure was so palpable that I lost all confidence in the message and in my gifts. I choked right there in front of the world.

You know that moment when you realize the agony on your audience's face is a result of them seeing the agony on yours? That's what I saw. I don't remember all I said, but I do remember what I realized. At that moment the truth set in: all these years I've been preaching for the opinion of men. It was eye-opening. It was painful. I was lost. I had no idea who I was supposed to be as preacher. I went inner-child for about three months.

You Can't Preach What You Don't Know

Entire books have been written on writer's block. How ironic! A writer would seem most likely to catch a bad case of writer's block while trying to wax eloquent on writer's block. Who stays inspired long enough to finish a book about that? Writer's block is that legendary phenomenon that cripples the creative flow. Unable to find inspiration, writing stops. It's that ubiquitous scene of a man banging his head against a keyboard in search of the next idea or word. Nearly every aspiring or accomplished author has suffered from it at some time. Or so I thought. I came across one well-known author claiming to have never suffered from it. Not ever. That surprised me. In light of the numerous gifted authors who admit to it, his claim sounded arrogant. That is, until I heard his explanation. His reasoning changed my opinion and enlightened my perspective on both writing and preaching. It also helped me understand what happened to me in chapel that fateful day.

According to him, the secret is knowing what *not* to write. Writer's block is not a lack of ideas, but a lack of awareness. An awareness of who you are, including your gifts and limitations. Writer's block is actually writing above your ability, not running out of ideas. If you exceed your limitations, you'll struggle to know what to say. As this author pointed out, those suffering from writer's block are "singles hitters" trying to hit "home runs." They're over-reaching. This is why the literary community refers to writer's block as a "failure of ego." In the preaching business, we call that pride.

Writer's block occurs about the time ambition exceeds ability. You have to know yourself before you know what to write. If you know who you are, you'll know what to write and what not to write. It's counterintuitive, but understanding your limits doesn't hamper your effectiveness. It liberates it. As you become comfortable in your own skin, your confidence in your skill grows.

The same is applicable in preaching—especially in delivery. Knowing your limitations is the starting point. A man has to find his voice (and himself) to preach with a freedom of conviction blind to the opinions of men. You can't aim at being a version of the preacher you most admire. I realize this sounds contradictory in a book arguing for the stylistic elements of various expositors, but bear with me. A preacher must utilize and trust the convergence of biblical clarity, confidence in God's gifting and the cat-alog of personal experience in his life to preach with authenticity. You are who you are. You must embrace and be comfortable with how God has gifted you. Sinclair Ferguson refers to it as the preaching voice, "Our approach to preaching that makes it authentically 'our' preaching and not a slavish imitation of someone else."[16] He went on to issue this exhortation,

> *. . . the literary community refers to writer's block as a "failure of ego." In the preaching business, we call that pride.*

> *We ought not to become clones. Some men never grow as preachers because the "preaching suit" they have borrowed does not actually fit them, or their gifts. Instead of becoming the outstanding expository, or redemptive historical, or God-centered, or whatever their hero may be, we may tie ourselves in knots and endanger our own unique giftedness by trying to use someone else's paradigm, style or personality as a mold into which to squeeze ourselves. We become less than our true selves in Christ. The marriage of our personality with another's preaching style can be a recipe for being dull and*

---

16   Sinclair Ferguson, "Finding Your Own Voice," Unashamed Workman, http://www.unashamedworkman.wordpress.com/2007/09/18/finding-your-own-voice (accessed February 2009).

lifeless. So it is worth taking the time in an ongoing way to try to assess who and what we really are as preachers in terms of strengths and weaknesses.[17]

As I was discussing this concept with a colleague, Chuck Swindoll's name came up. Rumor had it the discovery of his own preaching voice was a break-through moment in Swindoll's ministry. If a man with such obvious effectiveness as a biblical communicator placed such a high value on this epiphany, it behooved me to pay attention. So I asked him to elaborate. This was his reply,

> *I meant coming to see, somewhat fully, my own unique "style" and finding comfort in letting that unfold in a natural, authentic manner. In other words, not trying to "be" or "sound like" or "look like" any other preacher. Once a man has come to terms with this, he is truly liberated, freed from the grip of others' expectations and/or comparisons. Each spokesman for God is lifted, fashioned, and then used by Him who called us into ministry. Being who I am without varnish and without hypocrisy brings freedom as I preach.*[18]

Another preacher I interviewed described the preaching voice as the amplification of the preacher's personality in the presentation of truth. Given the above discussion, this description makes immediate sense. The "style" of any given preacher should include the magnification of who he is as a person. Phillips Brooks' famous description of preaching fits well here: "truth mediated through personality." If a preacher tries to be someone or something he's not, the delivery will be inauthentic and he will show a lack of integrity. Matt Chandler, Pastor of the Village Church, went so far as to call it sin.

> *It's sinful for you to be someone other than who you are. It's an ungrateful wicked heart that says "I want that to be my role" or "I want my role to be this" or "I want my mantle to be this" or "I want my following to be this." It's a wicked heart that does not run the race marked out for them. That*

---

17   Ferguson, "Finding Your Own Voice."
18   Chuck Swindoll, letter to author, May 28, 2009.

you would not grow comfortable with what God has called you to do. That you would not grow comfortable with how God has made you.[19]

The "voice" of a pastor involves the whole person, not only his literal voice. It includes his deep-seated convictions and the general disposition of his soul. If you are preaching the convictions of someone else, your own will be stymied. If you try to mimic another's style, you'll never find your own. Because you are their shepherd, your people depend not only on your clarity in exposition, but also in your passion for the truths you exposit. The greater your freedom to express this in preaching, the greater the impact.

At an intuitive level experienced preachers know that what counts as authenticity for listeners has as much to do with the expression of their pastoral persona as with what they say. Most parishioners come to see their pastor's passions, convictions, interests, questions, sensibilities, and affirmations as familiar perspectives reflect[ing] the person's identity as a person of faith. Over time what gets communicated in the best preaching is the preacher's authenticity.[20]

Your people know when it's you. They know when you're merely saying something and when you have something to say. Your people are encouraged when they see the impact of truth in their shepherd's life. It has to hit you first. Like a sound traveling across a given space, the sermon is the impact of the truth in the preacher's life making its way across the distance of a week. When it arrives in the ears and hearts of the people on Sunday, it's powerful.

Preachers who arrive at this sort of freedom discover a newfound energy. Not only in their preaching, but also in their love for ministry. It produces a renewed enthusiasm for their calling and a contagious optimism in the hearts of their people.

---

19   Matt Chandler, "Hebrews 11", Southern Theological Seminary, http://www. sbts.edu/ resources/chapel/chapel-fall-2009/hebrews-11 (accessed February 18, 2010).

20   Robert Stephen Reid, *The Four Voices of Preaching: Connecting Purpose and Identity Behind the Pulpit*, (Brazos Press: Grand Rapids, 2006), p. 16-17.

Fundamentally, a man must *study*, *prepare* and *preach* with a sanctified disregard for the preferences of men. Again, I'm not encouraging
some childish rebellion against the norm. What I mean to encourage
is a central conviction; when it comes to style in delivery, there are
no norms.

Delivery is as diverse as the personalities preaching. This statement should
make us a little nervous. So let me add the qualifier that is probably
floating around in your mind. There are elements which must be in
place for preaching to qualify as *biblical*: proper interpretive method,
accurate explanation of the passage and appropriate application. This
is true without exception. The combination of these elements produces a similar tone in every truly expositional sermon. But this does
not mean every expository sermon or preacher will sound the same.
If they do, there's something wrong.

Where to Start: Answering One Important Question

There are a number of notable expositors I admire. During the
course of this project, I've had the privilege of meeting and dialog-
ing with many of them. I listen to them preach on a regular basis.
Part of my research involved listening to countless sermons from
nearly every preacher imaginable. Hundreds of sermons into the
process, I noticed something. The ones I most enjoyed and whose
messages had the greatest impact on me had very divergent styles.
Not one of them was exactly the same stylistically. While they all
fell into the same basic theological camp (conservative evangelical)
and were expositional in commitment, they were all extremely different in their delivery. Despite the diversity, I gravitated to these
men. Why? It was the integrity with which they communicated.
Their insights and emphasis were the product of who they were as
individual Christians and pastors. Their stylistic elements were secondary, compared to the power of their sincerity. They all had one
central stylistic feature—a voice.

You know it when you hear it—whether a sermon is the unloading
of a burden or the urgent delivery of truth. It's not just that you believe what the preacher is saying. It's also that you believe how much
he wants you to believe what he's saying. Or maybe it's the fact that
he does not care whether you accept what he has to say; he has to say

it. It's the kind of delivery that distracts you from your watch. When it's over, you know the passage. When it ends, you wish it hadn't. It all comes together in an enviable liberated combination of truthfulness, transparency, exegesis, insight, conviction, passion and love. It's more than a well-constructed speech. What you just heard was biblical truth rushing through the heart and soul of a man.

The question is: how do we get there in our own preaching? How do we push our preaching up and over this hill? Where do we start? I recommend starting with one essential question. A question I put before all those preachers we most admire. It was the first question—and sometimes the only question—I asked of everyone I interviewed. As it turned out, the preachers who were most natural behind the pulpit had a concise and immediate answer. The others did not. Arriving at this answer is the first and possibly the final step in determining who you are as a preacher. So here it is:

When you step into the pulpit what is it you intend to do?

I know the answer seems simple. But it's not. You're probably thinking, "Preach the Word!" Of course, "Preach the Word!" But you would not be reading this book if you weren't trying to improve on something. Most likely your exegesis is not the problem. Probably what you really mean is: "Explain the Word!" That's not exactly the answer this question is after. This question is aimed at authentic delivery, not merely accurate exegesis. Allow me to take a few more patented answers off the table.

Answer: Accurately explain the truth to God's people.

Reply: We know you want to accurately represent the truth through your explanation. That's obvious by your consecutive exposition. That's not the question.

Answer: Defend the truth.

Reply: Clearly. This is part of your role as preacher. But it's not an exhaustive definition of preaching. That's not the question.

The above answers represent theological axioms which underlie our preaching. If you have a tendency to answer in similar ways, chances are you misunderstand the question. So let me clarify.

We believe the Bible is divine in its origin. We believe this, therefore, we also believe the Bible to be true, literal, infallible and without error. We also believe it should be accurately explained. Furthermore, we believe the Spirit's power alone can translate it and transform lives by it. Additionally, we firmly believe our responsibility is to present it without distortion. What I'm asking assumes all this and then goes beyond it.

Now reconsider the question. Knowing and believing all this— when you preach, what is your chief aim? "When I preach, my primary aim is to _____." It's a far more contextually driven and personally penetrating question than you realize. It can engender a range of additional questions such as:

What do you want to accomplish through the accuracy of your exegesis, the clarity of your explanation and the use of your gifts?

What do you want to effect with the presentation of the Truth?

What do you want to help accomplish through the exposition of the Word?

For you, what constitutes a successful and authentic delivery of the Word of God?

The answer is bound up in both the theological foundations and the personal capacities/convictions God has given you. The answer to my original question (when you preach, what is your chief aim?) gets to the core of who you are as a preacher. If you answer it honestly, you'll realize one of two things. First, you may discover your current style and delivery don't match your heart and who you are as a shepherd. There's an awkward disconnect. Or you might also discover a greater harmonization of conviction and style exists than you first realized.

What I discovered in posing this question to some experienced preachers was the correspondence between their answers and who they were as individuals. Their answers were accurate representations of who they were as preachers. It correctly portrayed them stylistically. Here is a sample:

John Piper—"Expository exultation."[21]

John MacArthur—"I have only ever wanted to be clear."[22]

---

21 John Piper, "What I Mean by Preaching", Desiring God Ministries, http://www.desiringgod.org/Blog/1792_What_I_Mean_by_Preaching (accessed February, 2009).

22 John MacArthur, interview by author, Nashville, TN, February 6, 2009.

Chuck Swindoll—"The overriding aim at all times is to bring glory to God … specifically related to preaching, it is to help others realize how relevant God's Word is. I don't make it relevant … my task is to help others see its relevance."[23]

Allister Begg—"When you step into the pulpit, your chief aim is to proclaim Christ with clarity, conviction, and compassion."[24]

C.J. Mahaney—"As you prepare your sermons, ensure that at some point you give your church a clear sighting of Calvary. Keep this landmark firmly in your view."[25]

Regardless of whether you prefer their particular styles or not, their answers accurately represent the impact of their preaching. In other words, their preaching is authentic. They know who they are and how God has gifted them. It's that authenticity which God uses to accomplish His work in the hearts of His people. It's the consistency between their personalities and deliveries that draws people in and gives God's Word a platform in their ministry.

We may be tempted to hear these preachers and mimic what they do stylistically. That's a huge mistake. What you're hearing and what you're drawn to is the liberation of their voice. You have to find your own. You don't do this by watching someone else exercise theirs. You have to get the answer for yourself.   This takes courage.

So now it's your turn to answer the question.

---

23   Chuck Swindoll, e-mail message.
24   Allister Begg, e-mail message to author, May 12, 2009.
25   C.J. Mahaney, e-mail message to author, August 4, 2009.

I don't need fifteen hours to prepare a sermon. I can prepare a sermon in half an hour. I need fifteen hours to understand the text with clarity. It's hard to get to the point of clarity. You have to be driven to understand it. But, if you step into the pulpit with a substantially clear grasp of the biblical concept, it has a profound effect on how you preach.

—JOHN MACARTHUR

Chapter Two

Clarity and the Power of "Ah Ha!"

I pray that the eyes of your heart may be enlightened, so that you may know what is the hope of His calling, what are the riches of the glory of His inheritance in the saints, and what is the surpassing greatness of His power toward us who believe.
— The Apostle Paul (Ephesians 1:18-19)

To reflect means to give thought to something to such a degree that it brings some kind of realization — an aha moment. It takes an idea and lives with it until it is burned deep within. It takes a question and, like Jacob wrestling with the angel, does not let it go until some form of answer emerges.[26]
— James Emory White

The Point at which Every Sermon Begins

Sermons don't start when preachers begin preaching, but when they begin understanding. Sermons are born deep in the rigors of study, long hours before "word-smithing" becomes an issue. It's the discovery we live for, not just the delivery. We study not only to comprehend biblical facts, but also to force the Truth—by the illumination of the Holy Spirit deep into the crevices of our own soul. We yearn

---

26   James Emory White, *A Mind for God*, (IVP: Downers Grove, 2006), p. 65.

for the epiphanies which take us from hearing to seeing; a moment of realization which functions as a gravitational force, drawing all our scattered facts together into a simple comprehensible whole. This moment is the sublime joy of the preacher's life. How many times—after mining for hours—have we pushed back from our desks in wide-eyed amazement? We come face to face with the one thought which every other thought exists to support. From this moment forward all those independent details we've uncovered—background, syntax, context, definitions, theology—begin to find each other. We see the image in the mosaic. Sunday's sermon finally comes into view. It's the "Ah Ha!" moment. When details and delivery are first acquainted. As a preacher of old put it, "Those meditations which are in such a sense our own that are little mingled with names, authorities, citations, and other men's thoughts and words, are most valuable to us, and most useful to others. They are worth waiting for."[27]

No doubt delivery is taxing. It's a wringing out of our soul. Everything I've spent the week soaking up forced out in a moment. As Paul put it, "I will very gladly spend and be spent for your souls." (2 Corinthians 12:15) Who we are—especially our inefficiency—is out there for the world to see. It is a painful transparency of life which most will never experience. When the sermon is finished, so are we. Spent. Personally, I walk around dazed like one pulled from the wreckage of a near-fatal accident, miraculously unharmed. "What just happened?" "How did I get here?" Unthinkably, I head off down the same route to the same demise the very next week. It reminds me of the popular definition of insanity: To do the same thing over and over expecting a different result. There has to be such a thing as a calling; otherwise we're just crazy.

Say One Thing Well

As taxing as delivery may be, getting to the preaching event is inexplicably harder. (If it's not, there is something wrong with your definition of preaching.) Saying something simply is a discipline which requires every ounce of energy we have. I've been told it takes three-quarters

---

27   James W. Alexander, *Thoughts on Preaching*, (Banner of Truth Trust: Edinburgh, 1988), p. 60.

of the space shuttle's fuel to get it into space. The remaining quarter is more than enough to guide it around and get it home. Verifiable or not, it's a great description of the preacher's week. The majority of our energy is spent breaking from the gravitational pull of our own ignorance. Once we've slipped its grasp, things come a little easier.

I've been training laymen in hermeneutics and homiletics for fifteen years. Developing leaders and teachers is a foundational ministry of the church. Currently, there are forty to fifty capable men at Community who, with the smallest amount of guidance, could effectively teach the Bible in an adult Sunday school class or home fellowship group. By "effectively" I mean they probably won't bore people to death or unwittingly espouse an ancient heresy condemned by a fourth-century church council.

Every student entering the preaching course faces an intimidating final project. A fifteen to twenty-minute message delivered to their peers in a lab setting. Once delivered, a review of their sermon by the same audience immediately ensues. It's an extremely daunting venue. Harrowing even. I have only one requirement: say one thing. Say one thing and support it from the text. I tell them, "If you will simply stand up and say what you are going to say and then say it from the particular passage, I will give you an A." I don't care about skill in oratory or any other desirable homiletical feature. Just do that, and you'll get an A. I go so far as to help the students work through their text and develop their thesis. I tee the ball up, put the club in their hand and tell them where to aim. They just have to swing. I don't care if it ends up in the trees or only goes ten feet. As long as it's not resting on the tee when it's over. To this day, no one has made an "A." It's impossibly hard to do. Mulligans are freely and liberally distributed, but it takes a couple of swings. What's the real lesson? This isn't as easy as it looks.

> *Every student entering the preaching course faces an intimidating final project [sermon]. . . . I have one requirement: say one thing. Say one thing and support it from the text.*

I would argue that plainness is the ultimate goal of exposition. Make the truth clear and avoid confusion. Or put another way—say one thing. This requires discipline, time and practice. This digestible plainness is a key trait in the most gifted preachers of our time. The fact of the matter is good preaching doesn't just happen, but neither is it reserved for the uniquely gifted. To assume otherwise is to deny the Bible's testimony about the true source of effectiveness in preaching and delivery.

> *And when I came to you, brethren, I did not come with superiority of speech or of wisdom, proclaiming to you the testimony of God. For I determined to know nothing among you except Jesus Christ, and Him crucified. And I was with you in weakness and in fear and in much trembling. And my message and my preaching were not in persuasive words of wisdom, but in demonstration of the Spirit and of power, that your faith should not rest on the wisdom of men, but on the power of God (1 Corinthians 2:1-5).*

Don't get me wrong. The preachers on our podcasts are gifted, but what you hear didn't happen overnight. Their repertoire is littered with "duds" just like ours. Lots of them. So take comfort in their failures. But know this as well, those whose delivery comes off as effortless and whose explanations are the easiest to comprehend worked very hard to make that happen—not just that particular week but over years. More to the point, in individual sermons the hardest work always takes place days before it's delivered. Usually, it's in one very specific area—thinking. As one has said, "If a preacher will not—or cannot—think himself clear so that he says what he means, he has no business in the pulpit."[28]

The discipline of mind required to think through divine realities and understand them on a deep level is unlike any other. Based on what I've been able to observe, if you want to improve your preaching, start with your thinking.

Well-driven Nails

The notable expositors of our day share some common traits: efficient mental discipline and a determined capacity for reflection. As Solomon put it, they "ponder." They think really well and deeply. Is it not the finely-sliced nuance which creates the enviable dynamic in

---

28 Haddon W. Robinson, *Biblical Preaching: The Development and Delivery of Expository Messages*, (Baker: Grand Rapids, 1980), p. 39.

their presentation? They have the capacity to focus their minds on a singular topic or truth for the length of time necessary to penetrate the obvious and unearth the profound. When they do deliver their sermons they come across as "well-driven nails."

It's not uncommon to hear of expositors spending fifteen to twenty hours a week working through their text. In our circles, time spent in study is dropped as a verification of true commitment. In some unfortunate cases, this knowledge doesn't help. It only makes the congregation wonder what was done with all that time. Without a doubt, diligent study is to be commended. But it is only a portion of what makes for good preaching. It's not whether you spent fifteen or twenty hours in study. The real question is, "What did you do with those hours?"

The error is great in supposing that the mind is making no progress and acquiring no knowledge, when it is not conversing with books; and it is one of the errors of bookish men. There are pauses amidst study, and even pauses of seeming idleness, in which progress goes on which is likened to the digestion of food. In those seasons of repose, the powers are gathering for new efforts, as land which is fallow, and recovers itself for tillage.[29]

Your favorite biblical communicators are resourceful in contemplation. Their use of time is what makes the biggest difference between their preaching and ours. Study schedules and processes vary from one preacher to another, but in every case one thing is the same—everything about their lives is arranged in such a way as to give maximum attention to the one central thought being delivered to God's people in a given week. Their personal approach is well thought out, and their schedule is tenaciously and jealously protected. This is not because they're antisocial, but because they view the contemplation of God to be their chief responsibility and the primary means by which they love their people. As a result, they care deeply about creating space for reflection. A portion of their time is spent collecting the biblical data; the balance is spent focusing their hearts on acquiring the authorial intent, import and application of the text to their lives

---

29   Alexander, *Thoughts on Preaching*, p.63

and the lives of their congregation. Thesis and argument roll around in head and heart like a spiritual cud. What they're after (and know how to find) is the core. One author succinctly described what this looks like.

> *Finding the core means stripping an idea down to its most critical essence. To get to the core, we've got to weed out superfluous and tangential elements. But that's the easy part. The hard part is weeding out ideas that may be really important but just aren't the most important idea.*[30]

From beginning to end, they never stop reflecting on and weeding out that core. Even after the message has been delivered, they are still rolling it around. It's not just about input and output. The truth has become a part of the fabric of their souls. The results are undeniable. These men can preach.

To be clear, it's not their complexity that stands out; it's their simplicity. (Too often the most intelligent people I know are the hardest to understand.) The reason these gifted communicators have the ear of the average churchgoer, and the heart of Christ's disciples, is not because they offer complex thoughts. It's because they make complex thoughts accessible.

Usually, their most profound insights are the results of determined reflection. This is why—more often than not—we are impressed by the obvious things they point out. Really obvious things. Things we've never considered. Things we should have. Things we wished we had said. While listening to their preaching we often say things like, "I never thought of it that way before." It would be more accurate to say, "I never took the time to think of it that way." IQs and gifts are not (usually) the distinguishing factor. The difference is discipline of mind. What's the take-away? Personal clarity is indispensable to effective exposition.

---

30 Chip Heath and Dan Heath, *Made to Stick: Why Some Ideas Survive and Others Die*, (Random House: New York, 2007), p. 28.

John F. MacArthur

The Most Extraordinary Average Brain Expositor I Know

Clarity is the most important aim of the preacher's life. This is because of the nature of Scripture itself. Scripture is designed to reveal. It claims its own clarity. Therefore, the most foundational element of any biblical communication is clarity. Nothing happens without clarity. – John F. MacArthur[31]

Very early in my Christian life someone handed me a "MacArthur tape." That moment was God's Grace in my life. I don't remember exactly who handed it to me, but if I had the opportunity to thank them there's no way I could describe how important that one cassette has been. It was pivotal to my own spiritual formation and eventually my call to ministry. It introduced me to preaching. I have hundreds of cassettes to prove it.

As has happened with many others, "John" became my pastor. His preaching made the truth plain. At his best he is profoundly un-

---

31   John MacArthur, interviewed by author, Nashville, TN, February 6, 2009.

derstandable. His sermons and insights have shaped much of my understanding of what it means to be a believer. My own desire to preach was heavily influenced by John's presence in the pulpit. Back then I wanted to do what he did—explain the Bible clearly. He was then and remains to this day the best example of expository preaching I know. If John is anything, he is clear. This is not by accident; it's at the center of his life's ambition and calling.

Too many preachers have frustrated themselves and muffled their own voices seeking to mimic their preaching heroes. There is something disingenuous about a clone. If I had to guess, I'd say there have been more knock-offs of John's style than any other. Take it from someone who tried it in my early days, no one will mistake you for John MacArthur. His MP3s should come with a warning: "Sermon delivered by a professional. Do not attempt this yourself." There is only one MacArthur.

But this is not to say we should not seek to emulate him. There are features in his preaching that we should seek to incorporate in our own: his passion for demonstrating the sufficiency of Scripture through the act of preaching itself, his diligence, his courage. But if there is a single characteristic in John's preaching which every preacher should seek to develop in his own preaching, it's his clarity. I sat down with him over a weekend and tried to get in his head on the subject. In the process, he got in mine and reorganized my homiletical priorities.

The Importance of Finding it for Yourself

I don't need fifteen hours to prepare a sermon. I can prepare a sermon in half an hour. I need fifteen hours to understand the text with clarity. It's hard to get to the point of clarity. You have to be driven to understand it. But, if you step into the pulpit with a substantially clear grasp of the biblical concept it has a profound effect on how you preach.[32]

There's a reason John MacArthur sounds like an authority on the various subjects he deals with when preaching. By the time he's fin-

---

32   MacArthur, *Interview.*

ished preparing, he usually is. His research is the stuff of legend. Some of the insights he produces in the midst of his expositions are mind-boggling. Like when John exposited the twenty-third Psalm. It was like watching the *Learning Channel*. Everything you ever wanted to know about sheep. A professional shepherd from New Zealand was also present. When John was done the gentlemen said, "I had to come all the way to the desert metropolis of Los Angeles to learn something new about a subject [on which] I knew all there was to know." John has the remarkable ability to teach the most learned Bible student something new about the most familiar verses. MacArthur has a depth and richness in his preaching that is unique.

Where does all that stuff come from? According to him, it's basic. It's the result of an insatiable desire to understand the Bible for himself. All those remarkable sermons are the result of a basic question, "What does the Bible mean by what it says?" His love for God's Word is palpable. To sit and listen to him, in one way you'd think he was a new convert. He comes across like one of those people we love to have in our church, the one whose vigilant hunger and enthusiasm for the Lord and His Word has not yet been blunted by "churchianity." MacArthur's heart still burns deep within him (Luke 24:32) after all these years. I expected to learn about preaching and I certainly did, but I also walked away from our time with a deep impression of his life. The man loves Jesus Christ, so he studies. There's no secret skill. He's absolutely sincere, and that is why he's clear. He is "driven to understand."

> John has the remarkable ability to teach the most learned Bible student something new about the most familiar verses. MacArthur has a depth and richness in his preaching that is unique.

This discovery hit me between the eyes. The implication is hard to swallow. My inability—at various moments—to preach with simple clarity is not a failure in skill, but a failure in reverence. It means I don't yet believe what I'm saying to a degree which is obvious to my audience.

Let's assume for the sake of argument that personal giftedness is not what distinguishes John MacArthur from the "average" preacher. What is it then? It's a combination of personal passion and sincerity. Passionate sincerity or sincere passion. It's what drives him deep into the heart of the text and builds bridges to his audience. As I was sitting listening to him explain what he does, something occurred to me. What I've been listening to all these years is not just John's clear explanations. I've also been hearing his conviction and his heartfelt belief in what he's explaining. The combination of these elements has produced his trademark simplicity.

John is first and foremost a disciple of Jesus Christ. There is an underlying desire to discover the greatness of God and to know his Savior deeply. As an individual, he is supremely dissatisfied with superficial treatments and obvious answers and is incurably analytical and curious. These bents also mark his approach to studying the Word of God. Someone described John as "studying at the level of a scholar and communicating at the level of a friend." That's the best description I've heard thus far. He's a well-spoken scholar, or he's a well-informed friend. Either way, what may not be obvious is that this skill rests on a zeal for the things of God. Not ability, but zeal with knowledge. In a word, *worship*. John demonstrates that the quality of our delivery must rest not on cleverness, structure or personal skill, but on the integrity of our relationship to Jesus Christ.

Average Brains and Dead Germans

This sounds ridiculous, but John does not consider himself to posses a superior intelligence. When he mentioned this during the interview, my staff—lined up against the walls of my office listening in—laughed out loud. They tried to cover it with a cough and then apologized. John turned and looked at them but had no idea what was funny. He's not kidding. My initial response to John's self-assessment? If he's average, I'm in a cave banging rocks. Not surprisingly, his closest friends and associates disagree with his self-assessment. None the less, John is firm on this point. He views his "average intelligence" as a primary reason he's been able to connect with so many people. As he put it,

> To be clear it helps to have an average brain. It helps to not be
> too intelligent. I need a simple understanding of everything. I
> battle with the Scripture until I can understand it. There are

other very intelligent people who don't need to bring it down as far as I do.[33]

When you think about it, this makes total sense. Those who try to be profound aren't—they're just hard to understand. They appear awkward because they're trying to be profound. In contrast, the truly profound are straightforward and easy on the ears. Their primary ambition is not to impress, but to understand it for themselves.

To explain things in terms only elite scholars can understand is not impressive. It's boring and irrelevant. To explain things in a way that touches both scholars and mechanics is impressive, exciting and relevant. That's John's "gift." He studies to understand the text for himself. In so doing, he's able to explain it to anyone who asks or who happens to be sitting there—even the professional shepherd.

> *If there is a new convert from a Hispanic background who has just been converted out of Roman Catholicism sitting next to a seminary professor in the congregation, I want to make it clear to both. It's comprehensible to everyone. If you understand it well you can say it in such a way that even the person who knows the most gets something out of it.*[34]

A reviewer once described the MacArthur New Testament Commentary series as being useful for the "untrained layman." That's code for "no serious scholar would stoop to use them." John's response?

> *I took that as a compliment. I've spent my entire life talking to the untrained layman. I'm not talking to dead Germans, liberals or scholars in a PhD program. I'm talking to the untrained layman. More than anything, I'm talking to myself. I need a simple understanding of Scripture. I have to have it broken down into simple concepts. As it turns out, so does most everyone else.*[35]

"I'm not talking to dead Germans!" That's classic. In fact, it's a dem-

---

33   MacArthur, *Interview.*
34   MacArthur, *Interview.*
35   *Ibid.*

onstration of the very skill we're talking about—it says it all. I, along with countless others, thank God for the truth behind this particular criticism. Is it any surprise the MacArthur commentary series has had such a lasting presence? These wonderfully simple explanations are the result of painstaking treatments.

John's broad usefulness over these many years remains somewhat of a mystery to him. As he put it, "I don't know why people find me interesting. All I'm doing is battling for an explanation that makes sense to me. I suppose in making it clear to me I am able to make it clear to the layman."

It's no mystery at all. John answers another criticism in the same self-effacing way:

> *I've been accused of lacking application. I accept that accusation.*
> *It's true in part because my two main concerns are understand-*
> *ing the biblical idea with as much clarity as I can and realizing*
> *the spiritual implication to my life. I preach with the confidence*
> *[of] knowing that a spirit-filled believer will be impacted as God*
> *intended by making the idea and implication clear.[36]*

The importance of personal clarity in the preacher's task cannot be overstated. The "ah ha" moment is the most liberating of a preacher's life. Illumined clarity wrought through diligent study and meditation is the most important moment in the entire preaching event. It simplifies the process, draws out structure and clears a path to delivery. John explained this phenomenon by pointing to the example of his own preaching hero.

> *I once heard a historian describe the primary motivation of Martyn*
> *Lloyd-Jones as a striving to understand the overarching biblical*
> *idea within the text. More than anything, he wanted to grasp the*
> *greater concept and argument. That best describes me and is exactly*
> *what I do.[37]*

Fist Pumps in My Head
Several years ago I had the privilege of attending a discussion on homiletics where John was the guest lecturer. Since he's a living ex-

---

36   *Ibid*
37   *Ibid.*

ample of what we strive to do, the professor wisely let him talk. The format was question and answer. Early on someone asked for tips on finding the "plural noun proposition." John actually looked puzzled by the question. I'll never forget his answer, "I wouldn't waste my time obsessing over plural noun propositions, outlines and structures. Every passage is different. If it's not in there, you should not force it. Preach what's there. For me, every sermon is different. There's no template."

Basically, he advised us to "forget what you've been told about structure and delivery. Preach the Word!" The homiletics professor nearly died. I was doing fist pumps in my head.

I doubt any of us would have expected John to minimize a traditional homiletical structure, especially in view of his commitment to the expository method. This is because most of us assume the expository method has a particular style. Obviously, he did not mean structure is unimportant, but what he did expose is an assumption. When we think "expository," we immediately imagine a very specific type of structure and delivery. But there's nothing sacred about style in delivery. (As long as our style doesn't interfere with the Bible's message.) I know this makes us nervous, but I would argue that some of our so-called expository structures do the exact opposite of what we intend them to do. Instead, they obscure the message.

It's important to understand what John was getting at by his comment. There is something essentially important which precedes homiletical structure: Clarity. A deeply informed understanding of and familiarity with the passage leads to an organic structure rather than an artificial one. John MacArthur is a great example of this very thing. As he preaches, what he's come to know on a very deep level comes out in a symmetrical and textual arrangement. But that's John. It may not necessarily be you. Obviously, we must seek to present the truth "properly and in an orderly manner." But what's more important is that your heart has been filled with the meaning of the text before you stand and deliver. As John put it:

> I want to understand the multiple ideas within the larger and
> then the larger concept. You have got to capture the main idea

within a passage. When you are able to articulate that in a crystal clear fashion, the structure of your sermon is simply the way you make that message clear to others.[38]

While Out Walking the Dog

The reason we often feel panicked at the end of a week is not due to time, but space. Space to think. We don't know how to present (homiletics) what we have learned from the text (exegesis) because we have not given ourselves the space required to formulate it. If the sermon has not yet ministered to our own soul, then it's nothing more than a thesis paper. There are clearly defined moments of input and output in sermon preparation. We must do the work. Exegesis rightfully occupies the first moment, homiletics the last, but our tendency is to overlook the moment in the middle. The space in-between is where more than a well-structured display of our hermeneutics or some memorable moralizing happens; it becomes a sermon.

Even John needs this grace. An entire day of his preparation is dedicated to meditation and prayer. Or to put that another way, John spends an entire day zeroing in on what he's just spent the previous two days uncovering. As he does, he's praying, contemplating, reflecting, connecting, wrestling, rejoicing—and sometimes golfing.

Hermeneutics and illumination—theologically these two words could not be more conjoined. Usually, we fail to consider how their relationship affects what we do as preachers. But their intersection lies at the heart of true sermon prep and delivery; you can't have one without the other. If we put all our emphasis strictly on hermeneutics, then we're no different than dead liberals and their mechanistic mode of interpretation. As one author put it, "…it must be understood that unattended exegesis will not penetrate the human heart, accurate though it be." Conversely, if we concentrate strictly on illumination, then we're no different than modern experientialists with purely subjective methods. What saves us from failure on both sides is the combination. We labor in exegesis *and* the Spirit illumines.

Illumination is a work of the Spirit wrought in the heart of the

---

38   *Ibid.*

believer. Obviously, we don't cause this. At the same time, this work is formed in and *through* a mind submitted to the text. Illumination is underway not only in the moments of desperate prayer, but also in the quiet moments of contemplation. It takes place throughout the process. This is especially true with consecutive exposition. As John put it, "This is the genius of expository preaching. It is a thematic treatment of a text, assuming that it is part of a greater theme."

As we roll through those sections attached to that greater theme, the Spirit is drawing our understanding toward a more concise awareness. We're coming to understand more than what is obvious. We're grasping what is intended. The Spirit is putting the big picture together. He compacts the truth. Illumination is not a flare we send up when we're pressed up against deadlines, begging God for a miracle.

Illumination is not a flare we send up when we're pressed up against deadlines, begging God for a miracle.

> *Throughout this process the man of God prays. From beginning to end he asks for insight: 'Dear Spirit of truth, grant more illumination. I need more light. Make evident the meaning and relevance of your word.' Then, as the meaning of the passage becomes clear, it begins to grip the heart of the preacher. To him it may now seem the most important passage of all the Bible. Surely, the Holy Spirit has been operative.[39]*

I once read a paper on the relationship of hermeneutics and illumination. I say "once" not because it's the only one ever written, but because it might as well be. Despite the relationship, there's little available on the subject that is grounded in Scripture. "Illumination" scares us by virtue of its ambiguity. In the article, the author was treading on thin ice attempting to capture the experience of illumination in real time. I think he got close.

According to this author, the convergence of hermeneutics and illumination happens in that moment during a break in your study when

---

39   Arturo G. Azurdia, *Spirit Empowered Preaching: Involving the Holy Spirit in Your Ministry*, (Mentor: Great Britain, 1999), p.151.

you're out walking your dog. At the farthest point in your route, it occurs to you what Paul meant when he said "as to the righteousness which is in the Law, found blameless" (Philippians 3:6). Paul did not mean he had perfectly obeyed the Law. That would contradict the core of his message and the Gospel itself. He was getting at something more specific. The Apostle abandoned moralistic Judaism not because he couldn't hack it or because it was too demanding, but because it did not work. Paul was a rising star and at the top of his game when he turned in his credentials. As he put it, "If anyone has a mind to put confidence in the flesh, I far more" (3:4). His former peers, the "evil workers," were aware this accusation had no merit. All his achievements were well-known. Paul was no quitter. He abandoned his "dung heap" of self-righteousness because it would not save him. When he saw Christ, the heap made him sick. He fled to a righteousness outside of himself. As when Luther reached the top of the steps in Rome, it was all over. Paul's conversion was a devastating blow to moralists everywhere.

The next moment you're somewhere between race-walking and running. Your poor dachshund is stretched out on the leash like a windsock. You get back home, sit down at your desk and in the margin of your exegesis you write, "Paul was no quitter." This is what we "strive" for. This is clarity. This will preach.

Stuck in the Dead Zone

The struggle of expository homiletics has been likened to climbing a mountain. On the ascent side are all the various aspects and details of exegesis. We make our way through them on the way up. On the descent side are delivery and homiletics. We make our way through them on the way down. While each side poses its own set of obstacles, our greatest difficulty is getting from one side of the spectrum to the other. Getting over the hump. Some avoid the difficulty altogether and start on the delivery side without traversing the details. Their sermons are mainly creative motivational speeches with little biblical content. Even the passages they cite have little to do with what they are saying. How could it be otherwise? They skipped that part.

While we may secretly envy their cleverness, our consciences can't stomach the shortcut. We start where we should—with the text— and make our way up the steep side. But, borrowing from the analogy here, near the summit we usually get stuck in the "dead zone." That deadly place where we get disoriented, tired and stop moving. Any chance we had at a real sermon dies on the side of the mountain, within sight of the summit, buried in a drift of details. (Sorry about that. I got carried away with the image, but you get the point.) It's hard to get over there. As the saying goes, *move or die.*

Bryan Chappell, president of Covenant Theological Seminary and author of a tremendous work on expository preaching, has identified several important questions the student-preacher must answer in making the transition to the "other side" of the process. He explains their importance for the reader.

> *Prior to answering these questions, a preacher has information only about a text, not a sermon. Although many preachers may feel that when they have done enough research to determine the text's meaning they are ready to preach, they are mistaken. To this point they are only like "the little engine that could," chugging up the expositor's mountain saying, "I think I can preach. I think I can." Answering these remaining questions actually pushes the preacher over the crest of the mountain, converting textual commentary or an exegetical into a sermon.* [40]

Chappell offers these six questions:
1. What does the text mean?
2. How do I know what the text means?
3. What concerns caused the text to be written?
4. What do we share in common with those to whom the text was written?
5. How should people respond to the truths of the text?
6. What is the most effective way I can communicate the meaning of the text?

The first three are concerned with matters of the text itself. The remaining three with matters of delivery. The sequence of Chappell's questions leads to what he indentifies as the "fallen condition focus" or the *FCF.* The *FCF* is the "mutual human condition that contemporary

---

40   Brian Chappell, *Christ-Centered Preaching: Redeeming the Expository Sermon,* (Baker: Grand Rapids, 2005), p.105.

Christians share with those to or about whom the text was written that requires the grace of the passage God to glorify or enjoy him."[41]

Answering the above series of questions carries us from the starting point of the finest syntactical details to the finishing point of effective delivery. The logical flow of his questions proves very helpful. In fact, he's done the best of anyone I've read in identifying and solving this difficulty for expositors. Ultimately, every exegetically focused preacher works through some version of these questions whether he intends to or not. In my own experience, I've reduced the diagnostic questions to three:

1. What does the text say? (Exegesis)
2. What does the text mean by what it says? (Interpretation)
3. What was the author intending to effect in his audience? (Intent)

As in Chappell's list, the division occurs along hermeneutical and homiletical lines. The first two deal with exegesis and interpretation. What are the facts and what do they say? The third question deals with homiletics. It's this third question which gives us the best transition to delivery. It is *intent* which gets us to the other side. Walter Kaiser stated it this way, "The only proper place to begin then is with the human author who claimed to obtain his meaning from being in the heavenly council of God."[42]

What did the author intend? What was the author's purpose? According to the context, what was he seeking to accomplish with his audience? So it's not just what he said (1-2), but what he intended to address and effect by what he said (3).

> *Behind the meaning of the text is the author's intent. We need to bring every available tool to the task of understanding the text in its context—grammar and syntax, archeological and historical data...The author's meaning in the text must not be assumed to be always simplex because intentionality is not always simplex.*[43]

---

41   Chappell, *Christ-Centered Preaching*, p. 50.

42   Walter C. Kaiser, Jr., *Preaching and Teaching from the Old Testament: A Guide for the Church*, (Baker: Grand Rapids, 2003), p. 51.

43   David L. Larsen, *The Anatomy of Preaching: Identifying the Issues in Preaching Today*, (Baker: Grand Rapids, 1989), p. 160-161.

Consider the account of the resurrection in Matthew's Gospel (Matthew 28:1-15). It's obvious, even from a cursory reading of the text, that the author was defending the historicity of resurrection against various denials present at the time. A Pharisee, Joseph of Arimathea, retrieved and prepared the body. Not a Galilean sympathizer. The Sadducees sealed the tomb. They locked it and swallowed the key. They finally stationed soldiers outside. No way the disciples could get near it. The women in the story are also important. Their testimony would not be enough in this patriarchal culture to explain the biggest ruse in the world. If you were going to make this up, it seems you would create more credible witnesses.

There are other details like this in the text, but what's the overall message? The resurrection wasn't a hoax. It happened. But why did Matthew share all these details? Just to prove it was true? Obviously! That's part of it. But, he was not only defending it, he was also encouraging the Church to trust in it. He wanted the church to lean on the empty tomb despite the assaults of the world. He wants us to walk down to the tomb and touch its walls. While preaching this periscope, our homiletic should aim at this same objective. As we preach, we should not only explain the point of this text but also drive our audience to the same confidence intended by it.

Once we can answer the question of intent we can more easily think about how we want to communicate the same intent to our own audience. "The value of intent comes from its singularity."[44] By focusing here we can more easily "say the one thing well." Grasping the intent helps us arrive at the clarity described herein. It also gives us a starting point in our homiletic. Ultimately, our intent and aim in our sermon should match the author's. Our homiletics should not only be built on the biblical meaning, but where that meaning was aimed.

What we are usually struggling with in our sermon preparation is a way to say what we've discovered in the text. To get there we have to keep in mind what the author intended to accomplish in the life of his audience through his message. What gets us to the other side in

---

44   Heath and Heath, *Made to Stick,* p.28.

preparation is not the goal of transferring information, but duplicating the intended impact of the biblical author. Our homiletic should match this. We should first clarify what was said and then seek to accomplish—through our explanation and by our delivery—what was intended by the author. Viewing it this way helps us answer all the remaining questions. In fact, the other diagnostic questions become somewhat superfluous. Things begin to take care of themselves. We know what our audience's need is as we compare it to the original context. We know how they should respond as well. From that point on, our homiletic is more specifically about clarity.

Chapter Three

Depth and the Mind-blowing Effect of God

The essential secret is not mastering techniques, but being mastered by convictions. In other words, theology is more important than methodology... Techniques can only make us orators; if we want to be preachers theology is what we need.[45] *— John R. W. Stott*

To use the vernacular, it's mind blowing to focus your attention on who God is and what He is in His being and character. Most Christians spend little time on these questions. It bugged me to see the experience students were having examining the doctrine of God in an academic way. I felt like the laity of the Church was missing all of this.[46] *— R.C. Sproul*

The Depth to Which Every Sermon Should Go

I was fifteen years old when a friend gave me his personal copy of Tozer's *Knowledge of the Holy*. In a show of sincere love he helped push my faith toward a theocentric start. It may have been the first Christian book I read. I still own it. The book came with a dramatic endorsement from my friend, "This will change your life." There

---

45 John R. W. Stott, *Between Two Worlds: The Art of Preaching in the Twentieth Century*, (Eerdmans: Grand Rapids, 1982), p.92-93.

46 R.C. Sproul, interviewed by author, Orlando, FL, May 12, 2009.

aren't many experiences which fall into that category. We greatly overuse the expression, applying it to everything from technology to cuisine. (But I've never had a sandwich change my life.) What we usually mean by the expression is: "You will really enjoy this." But in this instance, my friend was being literal.

I took his gift on a family ski trip to Colorado. My conversion came complete with a new desire—*reading*. A stereotypical jock, I was not much into reading or thinking. When I eventually made the dean's list in college (my first and last time) my dad nearly died of a myocardial infarction. What speaking in tongues is for some, a desire for education was for my dad—a sure sign of real conversion. For my dad, a medical doctor, reading might as well have been a fruit of the Spirit.

I read all night. Highlighter in one hand, book in the other. One of those M.D. penlights between my teeth. It was my first exposure to Theology Proper and the attributes of God. I had no idea what it was called. I also had no idea what was about to happen. Stretched out on the floor of our Chevy conversion van, I came face to face with the most profound thoughts man will consider. It was the really esoteric stuff about God we're usually not exposed to until much later in our Christian education. Solitariness. Sovereignty. Infinity. Omnipotence. Omniscience. Eternality.

Never before having considered anything of this magnitude, my head nearly exploded. I would read. Stop. Highlight. Read. Stop. Highlight. Every new concept was overwhelming. In a good way, it was hard to bear. This continued until morning. I finally finished the book somewhere around sunrise near Amarillo, TX. Something struck me in the light of day—I had highlighted almost every line. It was a seminal moment in my life.

I entered that van with a stereotypical sentimental view of God. I exited a devastated worshipper. It was a crushing blow to the little idolater hiding inside theology. The experience is unsurpassed in my twenty-six years as a believer. I've been trying to relive it every day since. It changed my life. I believe the same mind-blowing depth of experience should be the consistent aim of all Christian thought and the proper goal of all biblical preaching. We need to blow people's minds with their God.

All these years later, I now have the distinct privilege of triggering the same theocentric landslide for others. As a pastor, I've never gotten used to the awesome moment when the "lights come on" for others. If that doesn't thrill you, you should go sell insurance. There's nothing quite as fulfilling as watching people lean slightly forward on the edge of their seats wrestling along with me as I put forth "big" doctrines of the Bible. I enjoy seeing them stunned. Bewildered is good. Overwhelmed is preferable. As C. S. Lewis noted, "God is no fonder of intellectual slackers than any

Stretched out on the floor of our Chevy conversion van, I came face to face with the most profound thoughts man will ever consider. . . . I entered that van with a stereotypical sentimental view of God. I exited a devastated worshipper.

other slackers. If you are thinking about becoming a Christian, I warn you that you are embarking on something which is going to take the whole of you, brains and all."[47]

He's right. There are scary doctrines out there. Doctrines which don't fit neatly into our brains. Thorny realities which mock our tidy little explanations. You can't protect your people from them. So don't even try. If they read their Bibles, they'll find them. Don't avoid these encounters; embrace them. Some would suggest certain doctrines are too controversial or complex to discuss openly or to be introduced from the pulpit, as they will only divide or confuse. The fact is that you can't simultaneously avoid them and faithfully preach the Bible.

A church that is committed to sound teaching will naturally process through the biblical doctrines churches too often neglect. To our eyes certain doctrines may appear divisive. Yet we can trust that God has included them in his Word because they are foundational for understanding his work in salvation.[48]

Personally, I've benefited from a congregation which openly wrestles with tough questions. They're comfortable confessing a certain amount of theological tension and open-endedness. On a number of occasions

---

47   C.S. Lewis, as cited in Piper, John, *Brothers We Are Not Professionals: A Plea for Pastors for Radical Ministry* (Broadman & Holman: Nashville, 2002), p.97.

48   Mark Dever, *What Is A Healthy Church?* (Crossway: Illinois, 2007), p. 72.

they've observed their pastor publicly admitting defeat. It's part of our collective sanctification and maturation process as a church. Together we're mooring ourselves to the greatness of God. The church needs to struggle with hard things, not dismiss them. The struggle is healthy for the individual as well as the group. Grappling with His greatness helps us get over ourselves. Spurgeon explains it well, "There is something exceedingly improving to the mind in a contemplation of the Divinity. It is a subject so vast, that all our thoughts are lost in its immensity; so deep, that our pride is drowned it its infinity."[49]

Explaining some doctrines is like standing people up at the edge of the Grand Canyon for the first time. It's stunning. It's beyond words. But, for them to appreciate and respect it rightly, you have to sneak up behind them as they stand there in wide-eyed amazement and give them a firm shove. That'll do it. Suddenly, they're small. Such should be the aim of our preaching. Theologically speaking, it's the moment people realize their true status in the universe: *insignificant*. Our God is frighteningly transcendent. Not manageable, as we've been led to believe. The preacher's job is to shove mankind toward the abyss of His greatness. As one author put it,

> *...no one goes to the Grand Canyon or to the Alps to increase his self-esteem. That is not what happens at those massive deeps and majestic heights. But we do go there, and we go for joy. How can that be, if being made much of is the center of our health and happiness? The answer is that it is not the center.*[50]

This moment of realization is of inestimable value to the individual and the church. The fear of God calibrates many things in our Christian life as nothing else can. There's a power in His gravity. It tunes worship, purifies service, unifies fellowship, sanctifies methodology and necessitates the Gospel. As a pastor, husband, father, counselor and friend, I believe the most loving thing I can do for someone is

---

49   Charles Haddon Spurgeon, as cited in Boice, James Montgomery, *Foundations of the Christian Faith: A Comprehensive and Readable Guide*, Revised in One Volume (IVP: Downers Grove, 1986), p. 27.

50   John Piper, *God is the Gospel: Meditations on God's Love as the Gift of Himself* (Crossway: Wheaton, 2005), p. 13.

give them a higher and more exalted view of God. Even if it is hard on the brain and self-esteem. When we're both *amazed* at His beauty and *humbled* by His grandeur, we're truly useful. It cleanses us of the layers of narcissism plastered on us by the culture. Of course, this focus is not without its collateral damage. There's a real consequence to standing near something so great—a diminished view of self. A very acceptable loss indeed.

The Deep End of God

All the momentary afflictions we face in life—even if we can't "fix" them—find their ultimate resolution in the nature and attributes of God. "And we know that God causes all things to work together for good to those who love God, to those who are called according to His purpose" (Romans 8:28-30). They're certainly not resolved by giving them undo attention or focusing on our inability to change them.

This is exactly the realization of the psalmist in the seventy-third psalm. In the first half of the psalm, life was unraveling. He had "well nigh slipped" (Psalm 73:2). The various equations of the retribution cycle were not working out as expected. He was a man in despair. Yet, by the second half of the same psalm, his perspective had undergone a complete reversal. "My flesh and my heart faileth: but God is the strength of my heart, and my portion for ever" (73:26).

What happened to the psalmist? Therapy? No. It was an encounter with God. "Until I went into the sanctuary of God…" (Psalm 73:17). He stood on the precipice of God's nature and became small. He was exposed to His greatness and came out with a radically altered perspective of himself, humanity and life in general. But—and here's what's important to notice—the source of his despair was still at large. The world was still messed up. The context which drove him to personal darkness had not changed. He had changed. All by looking headlong into something greater than himself—a sovereign God. A God who does not stop to ask man's advice as He governs the universe.

As quickly as possible, I want people's thoughts of God to overwhelm their concerns about life. I want to take people up, not bring God down to a manageable height. This point was highlighted in a discussion on Bible translations. A notable scholar put forth a principle which applies directly to this discussion. No Bible translation should serve to reduce God down for man. The job of translations is not to make God convenient. This is somewhat counterintuitive since we usually assume the opposite. Translations should lift man up to God. Such is the effect of clear doctrinal preaching. It lifts man up to the nature, ways and means of God. As it is, we spend too much time strapping God with man-centered descriptions bending Him down toward suburban "needs." What the church actually needs is to be stretched upward.

Sadly, doctrine has fallen out of vogue in the church. This is an inevitable side effect of marginalizing the Gospel. When the church is about the Gospel, doctrine is essential. When it's about anything else, it's secondary. At present, it sits like a tie in the proverbial closet—waiting to come back in style. It's not the current fad. Os Guinness put it this way,

Evangelicals were once known as "the serious people." It is sad to note that today many evangelicals are the most superficial of religious believers—lightweight in thinking, gossamer thin theology, and avid proponents of spiritual-lite in terms of preaching and responses to life.[51]

So we're stylish, but shallow. Our effectiveness depends upon our depth. As Al Mohler explains:

> *Every pastor is called to be a theologian. This may come as a surprise to those pastors who see theology as an academic discipline taken during seminary rather than as an ongoing and central part of the pastor's calling. Nevertheless, the church depends upon its pastors functioning as faithful theologians – teaching, preaching, defending, and applying the great doctrines of the faith.[52]*

Forty years of church growth philosophy has managed to drain off our true source of worship—a mind engaged with the greatness of God. We've been too fascinated with *the creature* to care about *the Creator.* John Piper accurately describes the popular attitude toward doctrine:

> *Most people today have so little experience of deep, earnest, reverent, powerful encounters with God in preaching that the only*

---

51   Os Guinness, *Prophetic Untimeliness: A Challenge to the Idol of Relevance*, (Baker: Grand Rapids, 2003), p. 77.

52   Albert R. Mohler, Jr., *He Is Not Silent: Preaching in a Postmodern World*, (Moody: Chicago, 2008), p. 23.

associations which come to mind when the notion is mentioned are that the preacher is morose or boring or dismal or sullen or gloomy or surly or unfriendly.[53]

The Church now squirms uncomfortably in the awkward silence of profundity. We don't know what to do with stillness. Again Piper gets it:

If you endeavor to bring a holy hush upon people in a worship service, you can be assured that someone will say the atmosphere is unfriendly or cold. All that many people can imagine is that the absence of chatter would mean the presence of stiff, awkward unfriendliness. Since they have little or no experience with the deep gladness of momentous gravity, they strive for gladness the only way they know how — by being light-hearted, chipper and talkative.[54]

We've been conditioned to turn our noses up at doctrine. It's almost knee-jerk anymore. Most eschew it as elite scholasticism. As if doctrine is only for the select few up in their ivory towers. But doctrine is not for the select few. It's right there in the Bible for all to see and enjoy.

Some view doctrine as inferior to the more important responsibilities of the Church. Duties like caring for the homeless and disadvantaged. But it's not inferior at all. It gives these duties greater meaning.

Or we may marginalize doctrine as archaic and irrelevant. After all, how can a concept like the hypostatic-union make a difference in day-to-day life? But it's not irrelevant. It's indispensably important to every aspect of life, especially the hypostatic union. One preacher noted:

Doctrine is found in life, and life in doctrine. Doctrine reaches into the nitty-gritty and raw places. It reaches into the bruised and battered places. It travels to in the innermost places of the soul. It makes its way through the narrow places of human existence.[55]

---

53 John Piper, *The Supremacy of God in Preaching*, (Baker: Grand Rapids, 1990), p. 51.

54 Piper, *The Supremacy of God in Preaching*, p. 51.

55 Robert Smith Jr., *Doctrine that Dances, Bringing Doctrinal Preaching and Teaching to Life*, (Broadman & Holman: Nashville, 2008), p. 73.

Regardless of how much we may malign it, we always come back to doctrine at the critical moments of our life. Trust me, if you're diagnosed with cancer you will not ask for your copy of *Your Best Life Now*, *The Purpose Driven Life* or any other Christian best seller. You'll dust off your Bible and proceed to drown your fears in the deep end of God.

Typically, that segment of the church downplaying doctrine seems to focus on one of two alternate emphasis—practical Christian living or cultural relevance. We're after better-behaved kids and/or social justice. You rarely ever hear of people ending up at churches because the doctrine is solid or the Bible is explained clearly. It's all about "relevance" and "application." According to the experts, to be labeled a "doctrinal" church is the kiss of death. People readily jettison the heady stuff in order to find more purposeful and contented lives. Unfortunately, we've gone and thrown the wrong realities overboard. As Tozer made clear:

> *A right conception of God is basic not only to systematic theology but to practical Christian living as well. It is to worship what the foundation is to the temple; where it is inadequate or out of plumb the whole structure must sooner or later collapses. I believe there is scarcely an error in doctrine or a failure in applying Christian ethics that cannot be traced finally to imperfect and ignoble thoughts about God.*[56]

The Problem with Christian Marriage Seminars

It's assumed by most evangelicals that doctrine plays little if any role in life's more important issues. Take marriage, for example. Our most popular books on the subject would indicate the need is practical and not theological. But is not biblical marriage dependent upon *the* central doctrine of our faith, the atonement (Ephesians 5:22-33)? Paul's discussion of marriage was merely an opportunity to emphasize the power of the cross in one important area of life. He was not using the death of Christ as an analogy of marriage. We've got it backwards. He was using marriage as an analogy of the cross. Marriage is—at its core—a living analogy of Christ's death. The power of the cross on display within the most intimate relationship on earth. Paul's point?

---

56   A. W. Tozer, *The Knowledge of the Holy*, (Harper Collins: San Francisco, 1961), p. 2.

You can't have a "better" marriage without understanding doctrine, especially substitutionary atonement.

There's thick irony here. How is it you can spend an entire weekend at a Christian marriage seminar and never hear the Gospel preached or the atonement explained? A substantial commentary on the Church, I'm afraid. Paul's marriage seminars were much different than ours. At his, all you heard about all weekend was the Cross of Christ. "Session One: The Cross." "Session Two: The Cross." "Breakout Session: The Cross." "Husbands Breakfast: The Cross." "Wives Luncheon: The Cross." So on and so forth. Maybe, if you were lucky, he'd mention "marriage" somewhere toward the end. Or maybe not. Doesn't much matter. When you left, you understood marriage. Whether a husband or wife, you knew your responsibility. The cross makes Christian marriage obvious. More to the point, Christian marriage should make the cross obvious.

In my nearly twenty years of pastoral ministry, I've never had a couple implode because they didn't have enough practical marriage tips. Usually, it implodes because tips are all they have. There's no cross. Never was. Ironically, Christian marriage seminars are part of what's wrong with Christian marriages.

The same is true as far as the argument of "cultural relevance" goes. All our clamoring for relevance has made us naive. If we assume we can win this Christ-rejecting culture with a hot meal and a smile or by adjusting our language to fit theirs, we're fooling ourselves. This is not to say these adjustments are not helpful. There must be a balance between compassion and truth, lest we make the same mistake the Pharisees made. Jesus said, "But go and learn what this means: 'I DESIRE COMPASSION, AND NOT SACRIFICE,' for I did not come to call the righteous, but sinners." (Matthew 9:13)

There *is* a place for hot meals. I also admit, whether by archaic verbiage or escapist triumphalism, the Church has a habit of walling itself off from the very people it was called to reach. If we're armed with precise doctrine only (and not love), we're isolationists—even

> *If we assume we can win this Christ-rejecting culture with a hot meal and a smile or by adjusting our language to fit theirs, we're fooling ourselves.*

combatants—but not evangelists. Some of our attitudes would indicate we believe that hostility is an effective evangelistic strategy. But it actually works better if you don't hate those you evangelize.

I'm a recovering separatist who grew up on the harsh edge of cultural fundamentalism. As a result, I respond like a livid ex-smoker when it comes to moralistic isolationism in the church. I can't stand it. Our Lord commanded us to extend the Gospel into the world in His name and by His power. I say, "Go nuts!" Climb up on a 55-gallon drum and preach. Find some pagan friends to love on. Find a yard to rake. Or, by all means, recycle. But, as you do, keep in mind that your love and compassion (and relevance) will not save them, any more than their beholding a tree will. Our love and compassion simply provide an introduction to the One who does save.

In order to be good stewards of our opportunities, we must understand some central truths. Better known as "doctrine." Otherwise, when the opportunity arrives, all we'll save people from is hunger. A congregation with a heart for the culture (and the lost) must also have a mind armed with truth. How else will we answer the questions or fill in the blanks properly? We have to know doctrine to be truly relevant. Our foundations must be laid deep. And a sandwich never hurts.

How to Speak Peasant

This frustration brings us to this observation. It's easy to blame the Church's indifference toward doctrine on the broad enemy of nominalism. When people yawn during our sermons, we assume it's because they're not serious about truth. When groups of people migrate to the seeker church down the street, we condemn them as superficial. This is a cop-out. The fact is they don't understand us. We're obscurant. The seeker movement capitalized on this apparent deficiency fifty years ago as they decried, "We're out of touch with the culture!" Their solution? Package "truth" in such a way that narcissistic suburban Americans will accept it. Brilliant plan. The results were devastating. Like modern day iconoclasts the cutting-edge church growth experts robbed the church of its true power—the God of the Bible. All these years later, the church's landscape now appears like a graveyard of pragmatic relics. We've tried it all.

When it comes to the oft-reported epidemic indifference toward doctrine, we expositors need to take a good look at ourselves. We are partly to blame more often than we would like to admit. We assume wrongly that modern Christians have a developed theological vocabulary. We put the doctrines of the Bible out of reach through our inability to explain them well or demonstrate their significance to our people. We're simply not good at making them come alive or drawing them out of the text in a way that people value them rightly. No wonder people flock to pabulum. Unlike the great reformer John Calvin, who encouraged his students to speak in the *familiar voice*[57], we obscure their application and relevance. We make them hard to appreciate, much less pronounce. We're the ones who are boring, not the doctrines we present.

Like the scholasticism of the Dark Ages, we create impossible gaps between the common man and the truth. As when the German peasantry was at the mercy of an incomprehensibly complex church and an elitist clergy. Everything was in *Latin*. This is the exact moment in history that Martin Luther stepped into the confusion and started speaking "peasant."

Luther's exchanges with his theological opponents were heated and often peppered with caustic language. His debate with Erasmus in *The Bondage of the Will* is legendary. In some instances, his expressions are blatant vulgarity. But Luther wasn't trying to be crude or offensive for the sake of being crude or offensive. He was restating and demolishing the sophisticated arguments of the Roman Catholic Church in a tongue the masses could understand. He made the most complex logical and theological argumentation—used to keep common people down—easy to grasp. Suddenly, the average person knew as much as the priesthood. Hence, the "priesthood of all believers." Luther was the common man's theologian.

I'm not advocating we undertake the same tactics as Luther, but I am advocating the same goal—give your people a functional theology through the exposition of the Word. This is no simple task. According to Augustine, getting your mind around God is like

---

57   T.H.L. Parker, *Calvin's Preaching*, (T & T Clark: Edinburgh, 1992), p. 139.

pouring the entire ocean in a hole with a seashell one scoop at a time. And this is the easy part. Once we understand it for ourselves, we then have to turn around and present it in such a way that not only exposes historic errors, but also demonstrates its application in real time. Definitions are one thing. Explaining the complex and essential theological matrix which our faith rests on in a "peasant-friendly" format is another.

In the past five decades, no one man has better explained and rightly represented Christian doctrine than R.C. Sproul. He's been putting the ocean in a hole his entire life. He's our generation's Martin Luther. Educating and defending the Church in a vernacular even the simplest mind can comprehend and the most sophisticated scholar respects. He's left a priceless legacy in his wake. No matter where the attack on the Gospel has appeared: liberalism, atheism, pluralism, or Pelagianism, R.C. has stepped in to push it back. He's the best example I know of a functional theologian. He has that quality so rare among theologians: *understandability*. A quality we all desperately long for and need.

R.C. Sproul

A Man Fluent in Latin and Common

Ligonier Ministries was established in 1971 to equip Christians to articulate what they believe and why they believe it. Our foremost desire is to "awaken as many people as possible to the holiness of God by proclaiming, teaching, and defending His holiness in all its fullness." Our vision is to propagate the Reformed faith to the church throughout the world.

In order to accomplish this goal, Ligonier endeavors to provide solid teaching that helps bridge the educational gap between Sunday school and seminary. By making Christian education materials available, Ligonier hopes to encourage Christian laypeople to be transformed by the renewing of their minds so that they will be equipped to serve the church and glorify God (Romans 12:2).[58]

Accompanied by two elders, I met R.C. Sproul at an Italian restaurant in Orlando where he enjoys lunch two to three times a week, a home away from home. The owners, cooks and waitresses call him by name (as he does them). Having arrived in town the night before, we ventured out to reconnoiter pulling up to the restaurant around

---

58 Renewing the Mind Ministries, "Ministry Purpose", One Place, http://www.oneplace.com/Ministries/Renewing_Your_Mind (accessed May 2009).

closing time. I approached a table of servers who were assembled discussing the day's damage. "Excuse me. We're supposed to interview R.C. Sproul here tomorrow at lunch and…" That's all I got out. "R.C.," they said, "the good doctor!" It was like Norm walking into *Cheers*. At that moment all my suspicions were confirmed. He is and forever will be the common man's theologian. A very accommodating man with a very easily unaccommodating intellect. Some people throw Latin phrases around to impress. R.C.'s usage is unpretentious and natural. He actually thinks in *Latin*. Praise God he also thinks—and speaks—in *Common*. R.C. Sproul is a treasure of inestimable value to the Church. He's been our resident theologian for forty-five years.

It was among the most impactful afternoons I've ever spent with any one person. You simply had to be there. The man is definitely from Pittsburgh. He spoke in that distinctive Quasimodo-like voice you hear on the radio, with a rough and leathery sort of refinement. He ordered for the group. We spoke to one another with food in our mouths. Our hands politely covered the contents discussing everything from gout to acting classes. There were guttural laughs, moments of pin-drop quiet and everything in between.

The effect of the day was similar to attending a Bible conference. When it's not necessarily the particulars that stick with you, but the overall impact. I think that's called indelible. The entire experience was very much along the lines of who R.C. is as a person—a Renaissance man. Scratch golfer (before the train wreck). Talented guitarist. Accomplished painter. Lethal philosopher. Skilled theologian. Incredible communicator. Faithful pastor. Ministry director. Prolific author. Gifted teacher. Undeniable scholar. Successful publisher. The list goes on. But from the moment we sat down, he made us feel his equal—his friends. This is exactly the thing he does better than any theologian I know. It was the reason I was in Orlando.

My discussion with R.C. was a veritable goldmine. Not only about theological communication, but about communication in general. I was surprised to learn how serious he takes it. I had come to the right place. I learned more about the principles of communication from him in our meeting than I had over my entire life. It's a personal passion for him and a subject to which he has dedicated a tremendous amount of thought.

At times in our conversation, R.C. appeared annoyed by the inability of preachers to effectively relay doctrine. His reaction to the church's theological ineptitude is like observing a coach's frustration after his team fails to execute a basic play. "We should know these things by now!" In recent history he's been pacing the church's sidelines with head in hands. We've definitely dropped the ball.

It's not just that he thinks what we say should be said *correctly*; it's also that we should say it *well*. His determination is due in part to the value of theology itself. The theological constructs we have the privilege of explaining to our people are the most important truths men will ever hear. The benefits of precision and fluency are incalculable. It behooves us to explain them as best we can.

Blowing the Church's Mind for Forty-five Years

Ligonier Ministry has been a staple of evangelicalism for four decades. Surprisingly, its central audience has not been the classroom but the pew. It's unusual for ministries dedicated to upper-shelf theological instruction to be so popular among the "laity." Ministries devoted to the "propagation" of the "Reformed Faith" don't usually hold the attention of the church. We have a notoriously short attention span. But, for some reason R.C. has always connected. There are similar faithful voices out there, but none with quite the same breadth of impact. To understand why and what sets R.C. apart, you have to go back to the beginning. Back to some important experiences which serve as the genesis of his personal passion. These moments would drive him to hone the skill we observe today and set the course of his professional career.

As a senior philosophy major in college, he took a course jointly with the science majors: *The Philosophy of Science*. Out of the forty students in the class, only four were philosophy majors. The rest were studying various other sciences. The top thirty-five students of the graduating class were present. R.C. described it as the *crème de la crème* of the student body. The four philosophy majors aced the course with complete ease. But to his surprise, the physics majors, biology majors, chemistry majors and pre-med students struggled to pass. Without the ability to depend on the empirical processes of observation and experimentation, they were adrift. They had no capacity for abstract inquiry.

R.C. could only watch in frustration. He placed the blame squarely on the professor's inability to communicate the material. It was not a matter of the students' intelligence or lack thereof. They were smart enough. The problem was twofold: the professor's lack of command of the subject and his lack of concern for the students' comprehension. The professor was in the way of the material. R.C. walked out of that class and into the Church with one fundamental goal: get out of the way.

As has been stated, it's too easy to assume the problem is our people's lack of understanding. This is a fundamental mistake of the preacher. It's a self-righteous excuse. Humility compels us to start by examining our explanations. We have to blame ourselves first. The problem is not usually their lack of comprehension, but ours. We don't understand it ourselves and, therefore, we're in the way. We also can't assume it's a lack of appreciation. That mindset lacks compassion and is full of pride.

It wasn't long before R.C. found himself facing the same situation from the other side of the desk, as a college professor teaching philosophy to incoming freshmen. It was here he first cut his teeth on theological instruction.

> *What happened there had an impact on me for the rest of my life. I first taught philosophy before I taught theology. Philosophy is a particularly difficult subject. Intensely abstract—requiring an extraordinary use of logic to follow the abstract arguments of the various philosophers of history. People approach theological inquiry in different ways. Not everyone can relate well to that type of information.*[59]

As God would have it, at the same time R.C. was asked by his pastor to teach an adult class on the person and work of Christ. The class was comprised mostly of professional people. Suddenly he was faced with teaching complex concepts to two completely different audiences.

During the week his audience was populated by captive students. He could be as technical as he wanted because their presence and

---

59   Sproul, *Interview.*

participation were required. But on Sunday his audience was voluntary. "They had no background in theology, but they did have an interest to know the things of God."[60] Their presence was not a requirement. It was a need.

As it turned out, communicating at a lay level took far more skill than at the collegiate level. The point? It takes a greater level of expertise to simplify. Despite the fact that R.C. had always planned on being a "battlefield theologian" in the academic world, his passion for the laity and their passion for God drew him into the church. While fulfilling both obligations, he found his calling.

> During the week I found was getting bored. And on Sundays I was getting excited because the people were responding with so much excitement themselves.... When I would be teaching The Doctrine of God in the seminary classroom—the most abstract theological concept within systematics—going into depth on the attributes of God, I discovered something would happen. The students' grasp of the being and character of God would be elevated to a degree they had never experienced before. It would have an almost palpable impact on them—both in their responses and their Christian growth.[61]

It was here Sproul set out to "bridge the educational gap between Sunday school and seminary." It was here he aimed his life at providing both factory workers and doctors the same life-altering realizations at the same time. As he put it, "It bugged me that I would see the spiritual experience the students were having as they examined the Doctrine of God in an academic way. The laity of the Church was missing all this. I mean who preaches on the nature and character of God?"[62]

R.C. answered this question with his very life. The combination of these contexts over the years has created that uncanny capacity to speak to any level of intellect on any theological subject at any given time. As R.C. explained, "I have always had one leg in the academic world and the other leg in the laity."[63]

---

60   *Ibid.*
61   Sproul, *Interview.*
62   *Ibid.*
63   *Ibid.*

In a sense, our responsibility is the same. We should preach with one foot in the things of God and one foot in our people's living room. R.C. concisely described the basic challenge of his teaching experience. He was "teaching philosophy to people who had no intention of becoming philosophers."[64]

Our challenge as preachers is only slightly different. We teach theology to people who don't realize they are theologians. By definition theology is the "study of God." Therefore, every believer is a theologian by trade. Our job is making it both obvious and enjoyable.

Tipping Over Idols

We're idolatrous by nature. Our thoughts of God are all over the page. We start our journey far removed from the center. We could all use a theocentric shove. Part of our responsibility as preachers is to push the popular idols over on their faces. We topple them through a clear explanation of the Bible. As we preach, we confront our people's (and our own) misunderstanding and misrepresentation of God. From time to time, they let us know when we've stepped on a theological toe. Their sensitive reactions are often cloaked in traditional verbiage—*"I've always been taught…"* This is a sure sign of an internal debate. Challenges show up in questions you get via e-mail or face-to-face at the end of a sermon. It's to be expected. After all, it's not easy for someone to admit Grandmother was a heretic.

These are the moments we need to step in and speak *Common*. We teach with our feet planted firmly in both places—the Word and the office cubicle. Or wherever our people may be standing at the time. It's here that simplicity is so important. One author put it this way:

> As doctrinal preachers we need to be liberated from the sterile
> and predictable language used in our preaching. This language
> is more like dusting plastic flowers than cultivating roses. The
> doctrinal preacher needs to use language that is similar to the
> Bible – language that has elasticity and portability for use in
> our contemporary times. Doctrine does not come to us from some
> esoteric arena; rather, it emerges from the seams of society.[65]

---

64   *Ibid.*
65   Robert Smith Jr., *Doctrine That Dances*, p. 73.

Your people are *unintentional theologians*. Whether they realize it or not, they constantly grapple with life's most substantial questions. The same questions ivory tower scholars wrestle with. Let them ask. Force them to ask hard questions by faithful exposition. When they ask, get out of the way (with as much clarity as you can muster) and let them deal with the broken little pieces of their sentimental theology.

To do this we must be gripped by the same motivation as R.C., blowing the church's mind with God. We too often miss this opportunity by distorting even the easiest concepts. Confusion isn't hard. I mess up the announcements every Sunday. Imagine what I can do with the doctrine of election. I know when I've sailed over my people's heads. As R.C. pointed out, "it's that deer in the headlights look." Portable doctrine is challenging. Regardless of how hard we try, we often fall short in our explanations. But take heart because even the most difficult concepts can be easily explained. It only takes hard work.

Simple is hard.

The unsuspecting layman would be surprised to know the battles which are waged just to render average sermons and minimal concepts. It can be gut-wrenching. As the saying goes: "Being difficult to understand is easy. Being easy to understand is difficult." R.C. noted, "By simple I don't mean simplistic. Simplistic is shallow. Simple is not."[66]

To be simplistic, you need only to regurgitate facts. It's a restatement of the obvious, a running commentary and a flawless impersonation of a human tranquilizer. To be simple requires a very deep level of awareness and conviction which may be attained only by pushing ourselves beyond the limits of our basic understanding. Simple is a "pocket-sized" explanation of the profound. It's saying one thing—which may be complex in and of itself—in a way that anyone can grasp. Simple is not as easy as it looks. As has already been said, clarity begins with your own understanding. R.C. put his own spin on this critical idea:

> "Being difficult to understand is easy. Being easy to understand is difficult. . . .
> By simple I don't mean simplistic. Simplistic is shallow. Simple is not."
> — R.C. Sproul

66   Sproul, *Interview*.

> *If you don't have the ability to explain the concept to a six-year-old kid then you don't really understand it yourself. In other words, to simplify without distorting requires a very deep mastery of understanding of your content. And so, if you understand it then you can communicate it. If you don't understand it, you can just transfer information from your notebook to the next generation.*[67]

This gives me a newfound respect for Sunday school teachers, not too mention six-year-olds. But the truth of this observation can't be denied. It's easy to assume our people's glazed expressions reveal their inability to understand. In reality, the problem is our understanding, not theirs. When we cannot explain it clearly, we simply don't understand it. When we understand it, so will others.

What Everybody Thinks They Already Know

No one exemplifies this principle more so than R.C. He has a way of presenting not only the meaning of a doctrine but also its importance. In a few minutes, he can peel away the layers of misunderstanding which have a way of inhabiting complex doctrines. He exposes the point of our misunderstanding and tweaks it. Many of his explanations are not only concise but shrewd. We see not only what we should understand but how we've misunderstood it.

At one particular conference, I watched him expose an entire audience's collective misapprehension of imputation and justification. What made it all the more impressive were the events occurring in evangelicalism at the time. *Evangelicals and Catholics Together (ECT)*, a document calling for co-belligerence between Roman Catholics and Evangelicals, was being signed by a surprising number of conservative evangelicals. The Protestant world was ablaze with responses decrying the incongruity of the union. All at once everyone was an expert on the Protestant doctrine of justification and its incompatibility with Rome's view.

R.C. took the podium and declared, "I believe you are saved by works! You cannot be saved without them. To think otherwise is to deny the biblical Gospel." You can imagine the response. People were

---

67   Sproul, *Interview.*

baffled. He let the visible reaction go on for a moment and then said, "Not my works, of course. The works of Christ."

Sproul is tricky. There was a faint grin on his face. I went around for a month putting that one over on people. In the midst of the hysteria regarding *ECT*, we forgot that righteousness (works) is an indispensable condition of our salvation. The real question is "Who meets the condition?" It's certainly not us. Our debate with the Roman Catholic Church isn't about the need for righteousness but the means by which it is acquired. Sproul's method was brilliant. In that moment, I came to fully understand the doctrine of justification. So did the audience.

There are so many places this type of adjustment could radically enhance our people's understanding of basic doctrines. These counterintuitive reminders are powerful. Take *Christology* for example. In one way or another, every New Testament book is a defense of Christ and His nature. The opportunities to deepen our congregation's understanding of the Savior are limitless. This is true even with a perplexing doctrine like the *kenosis*.

Most people misunderstand what Paul meant when he says Christ "emptied himself" (Philippians 2). They assume it means Christ laid aside His divine attributes when he took on humanity. They understand "emptied" to mean "dispensed with." As if he left His deity in heaven, abandoning such attributes as omniscience and omnipotence. Such a view is touching but incorrect. According to Scripture, it could not be farther from the truth. "For it was the Father's good pleasure for all the fullness to dwell in Him" (Colossians 1:19). "And He is the radiance of His glory and the exact representation of His nature, and upholds all things by the word of His power." (Hebrews 1:3) He is fully God and fully man. By "emptied" Paul was pointing to Christ's selfless sacrifice and obscurity in death, not the abandonment of His divine attributes. He became nothing.

This is such a crucial modification. When we understand this, Christ's act goes from merely touching to infinitely more than we ever imagined. His sacrifice is far more remarkable when we realize His divinity was at His disposal. An incredible rebuke to our unlimited capacity for self-defense. Christ could have vacated this planet the first time his stomach rumbled from hunger, not to mention that He could have turned stones into bread. This is the very point the Apostle was making when he said that Christ, "although He existed in the form of God, did not regard equality with God a thing to be grasped" (Philippians 2:6). He never used any of His divine attributes to lessen the demands of God's righteousness or soften His suffering. The only time he ever employed His divine power was to serve others. His humility is infinitely greater with this in mind.

> *Then Jesus said to him, "Put your sword back into its place; for all those who take up the sword shall perish by the sword. Or do you think that I cannot appeal to My Father, and He will at once put at My disposal more than twelve legions of angels? How then shall the Scriptures be fulfilled, which say that it must happen this way?" (Matthew 26:52-54)*

"I Don't Know" Never Hurts

R.C.'s rhetorical capacities go way beyond the bounds of this work. If you've ever seen him in person, you know what I mean. He is a well-trained, extremely skilled and vastly experienced communicator. Yet, it's here I learned the true source of effective theological communication—*humility*. Dr. Sproul has never assumed his usefulness has anything to do with his competence. His *theology* won't let him go there.

> *When I step into the pulpit I have a fundamental feeling of helplessness. The Spirit must accompany the word with power. Anything I bring is futile unless the Spirit accompanies it. My job is to be as accurate as I can be in my understanding and as dynamic as I can be in my presentation. But I have no confidence any of that will have any impact. It depends on the Spirit. It will have no effect otherwise.*[68]

I really wish he hadn't said that. Helplessness? Really? To realize a man of Sproul's ability feels helpless is extremely humbling. To hear him admit the futility of his capacities is embarrassing for the rest of us who are so busy drawing connections between our level of pre-

---

68   *Ibid.*

paredness and our effectiveness in the pulpit. It's too often about us. We should work hard, but we should never forget where real power comes from. Honestly, after forty-five years of practice, who is more prepared than Sproul?

> *I know enough theology to know it does not matter how gifted I may be. It does not have any power. You may fascinate people. You may interest people. People may respond to your preaching, but it won't penetrate into their souls unless the Spirit accompanies it.*[69]

When I asked if a "fundamental sense of helplessness" was a necessity for every preacher, he quipped, "It would help. But honestly, there are guys who are helpless even with the Holy Spirit!"[70]

R.C. is humbled by all he knows, not puffed up. This makes perfect sense given that humility of mind is the starting point and inevitable outcome of all sincere theological inquiry (Proverbs 1:7). Particularly, a reformed soteriology. It's troubling to watch Calvinists—especially those who have recently discarded Arminianism—pridefully shove Reformed theology down the first throat they find. It's the exact opposite effect one should expect. A condescending or elitist attitude will always get in the way of simplicity.

R.C.'s teaching comes with a lowliness of mind rare among learned theologians. It's partly this absence of smugness and arrogance that draws people into his explanations. A gracious humility of mind comes through in all his theological inquiry. This is true even when facing theology's most taxing questions. When dealing with the fall of Adam and Eve in the garden R.C. remarked,

> *We are fallen creatures. But Adam and Eve were not created fallen. They had no sin nature. They were good creatures with a free will. Yet they chose to sin. Why? I don't know. Nor have I found anyone yet who does know.*[71]

While discussing the sovereignty of God in salvation—why some are saved and others aren't—Sproul admitted his limitations once again:

---

69   *Ibid.*
70   *Ibid.*
71   R.C. Sproul, *Chosen by God.* (Tyndale: Wheaton, 1986), p. 31.

The only answer I can give to this question is that I don't know. I have no idea why God saves some but not all. I don't doubt for a moment that God has the power to save all, but I know that he does not choose to save all. I don't know why.[72]

We should take our cue from R.C. Sproul. Our congregations need to observe the same type of honesty in us. Admitting intellectual defeat before the greater mysteries of God will not reduce our people's respect for us as much as it will increase their reverence for God. It fosters a corporate humility. Putting our hands over our mouths, like Job, at these moments is really good theology. This is not to suggest reasonable answers to tough questions don't exist, but a certain amount of mystery is healthy. A well-placed "I don't know" every now and then communicates more than we can imagine.

Ask This Question: Where's the Drama?

We pass by so many jaw-dropping moments. Not just the obvious ones but the subtle ones as well. We miss opportunities to blow our people's minds with their God. We fail to spot the theological movement in the passage and draw our people up to His greatness. Sometimes we're too quickly running past them to get to "application." We sprint right past truths which beckon us to stop and ponder. Or our systematics is unrefined. Our lack of awareness allows the connections to get away.

R.C. has spent the majority of his life teaching systematic theology. Over the last decade, he's been practicing consecutive exposition. This raises a legitimate and often asked question? What role should theology play in our exegesis? At what stage does it come in? Obviously, exegesis precedes systematics. It's the natural order of things. But part of our responsibility as exegetes is making the theological links obvious. It's a part of defending the Truth and enlightening our people. This is why R.C. proves to be such an example. All those years teaching theology have given him an eye for it in the text.

But the question remains: How do we make the theology in the text come alive without violating the priority of exegesis? R.C.'s

---

72 Sproul, *Chosen by God*, p. 37.

answer? Look for the drama. As he stated, "There's drama in every text." That is, there's a context, circumstance and intent underlying the passage. The passages we study to preach were written to real people in real circumstances.

Regardless of the genre, each text was written to a certain situation to address a certain need, relay a certain lesson or capture a particular moment of God's providence. There are so many theologically dramatic elements in every section of Scripture that you couldn't exhaust them in ten sermons, much less one. As R.C. pointed out, "There is enough drama in one day of your life to write a five hundred page novel. It only depends on how well you pay attention." Our job is to pay attention in our study.

Often we are so deep in the details of exegesis that we fail to notice the actual point being made by the biblical author. A frequent struggle of expositors is the failure to appreciate the forest by staring at knots on trees. This kind of near-sightedness greatly affects delivery. We never get to see the details we unearthed at ten feet from the perspective of thirty thousand. There's no awareness of the greater biblical theme or argument which holds the details together. The pieces of the sermon are like the pieces of an unassembled bike. Interesting but useless. This is where people struggle to follow us. That greater context (or drama) is like the picture of the bike on the box it came in. It helps us keep the final product in view.

Chip and Dan Heath make this very point in their helpful work, *Made to Stick*. They tell the story of how one successful author learned the lesson of paying attention early on in a high-school journalism class. On one particular day, the teacher had the students write a newspaper headline based on some specific details handed out in the class. Their job was to examine those details and then relay the main emphasis through a succinct and brief statement. As these authors tell the story,

> *The teacher reeled off the facts: "Kenneth L. Parker, the principle of Beverly Hills High School, announced today that the entire high school faculty will travel to Sacramento next Thursday for a colloquium in new teaching methods. Among the speakers will be anthropologist Margaret Mead, college president Dr. Rob-*

ert Maynard Hutchins and California governor Edmund 'Pat' Brown."[73]

The results were typical with students writing some version of: "Governor Pat Brown, Margaret Mead, and Robert Maynard Hutchins will address the Beverly Hills High School faculty Thursday in Sacramento… blah, blah, blah."[74]

After the teacher sampled the papers he surprised everyone by declaring, "The lead story is 'There will be no school next Thursday.'"[75] The impact was indelible:

> *It was a breathtaking moment… In that instant I realized that journalism was not just about regurgitating the facts but about figuring out the point. It was not enough to know the who, what, when and where; you had to understand what it meant. And why it mattered.*[76]

Because we're dealing with divine realities and the ever-present epoch of God's providence and grace, every detail leads to a breathtaking reality. It's not just the journalistic "who, what, when and where." There's also *why*. And it's the *why* we're after. The context of a particular provides the opportunity to show the importance of a given doctrine.

As one author points out, this raises significant *Hermeneutical* and *Epistemological* questions for some.[77] But if we assume God intended to deliver a message to a specific audience and that audience was able to understand it, then we too should be able to get *nearly* that same meaning and message through diligent study.

Consider the episode of Jesus healing the paralytic in Luke 5:17–26. I've had interruptions while preaching: a crying baby, a cell phone, but there's nothing quite as distracting as an acrobatic paralytic. Imagine

---

73   Heath and Heath, *Made to Stick*, p. 75

74   *Ibid.*, p. 75.

75   *Ibid.*, p. 76.

76   *Ibid.*

77   Kevin J. Vanhoozer, *Is There Meaning In This Text?: The Bible, the Reader, and the Morality of Literary Knowledge* (Zondervan: Grand Rapids, 1998).

teaching a home Bible study and you hear the shuffle of feet on the roof, a sudden burst of light from outside and a makeshift chimney appears. From the dusty whole in the roof, a crippled man on a pallet is lowered down to the floor. No way it was a synchronized decent like Hollywood might portray. No doubt he was crudely joggled downward until he was deposited on the ground, hung up like a marionette, at the feet of Jesus. It would be impossible to ignore. Sermon interrupted.

I can imagine the scene just before this moment. The helpless man is hurriedly transported across town by a crude ambulance of arms and hands. "Can you please take me to Jesus." And off they go running through the streets with their friend in tow. Why the roof? Space issues. It was standing room only to hear Jesus. Upon arrival the paralyzed man hears the disappointing news, "Sorry friend, it's packed. No way we're getting in there. Maybe next time." I can see the desperation in his eyes as he begs, "If you love me, you'll get me in there to Jesus." With that they scale the walls and make their way onto the rickety first-century roof. He's hoisted up and dragged over to right above the sound of Jesus' voice. They start "digging" for his life pulling up tiles.

It's a truly awesome scene. This story will preach. However, most times I've heard it preached, the point of the story has been missed. Usually, the sermons I've heard are on the importance of friendship or what sacrificial service looks like. In other words, we moralize the real story into oblivion. No doubt, these are faithful friends. Jesus even acknowledges their faith. But *their* faith is not the point. The object of their faith is the message. The point of it all—*the drama*—is found in the counterintuitive exchange that takes place between the paralytic and Jesus. Just reread it, and you'll see what I mean.

When he shows up at the feet of Jesus, the reader fully expects the Lord to say, "Get up and walk." A paralytic has just been placed at his feet in dramatic fashion. He's healed thousands of people. We're conditioned by the Gospel to expect this same outcome here. We also assume the young man's greatest concern is his physical condition. Why else would he be here? Isn't it what we'd be most concerned about? Jesus' reply proves each of these assumptions wrong.

Jesus says to him, "Friend, your sins are forgiven you." It's unexpected. If viewed out of context it can appear cruel. But Jesus knows what's on his heart. The context proves this as well (5:22). We can only conclude from Jesus' declaration that the man's real concern was not his paralysis, but his status before God. Given his culture's emphasis on retribution, it's quite possible he viewed his condition as some sort of judgment from God. That is—his paralysis was a demonstration of God's disfavor.

With no physical capacity to participate in the ceremony or fulfill the requirements of Israel's religion, the man would be left to suffer intense doubt. He would be weighed down (more than most) by the peculiar anxiety of moralism. He was helpless. No merit. No labor. No works. No credentials. He was reduced to putting his trust in Christ. All he had was faith. What a great place to be.

In other words, he's a perfect picture of *Sola Fide*—justification by faith alone. Which is the point (5:24). It's proven by the leader's response. They immediately object: "Who is this man who speaks blasphemies? Who can forgive sins, but God alone?" Two observations come into view. First, they had no idea who Jesus really was, God Himself. Ironically, they unwittingly answer their own question. Secondly, the idea of immediate justification blew a whole in their sky. It was an impossible concept for them to grasp. Who could be made righteous in a moment? What of works? What of man's merit? It could not be that easy. Like Nicodemus who begged the same questions in his late night debate with Jesus, "What about all this stuff I've done?"

In order to put the leaders in their place and prove both his deity and authority, Jesus instantaneously heals the man of his crippling condition. Literally, the guy gets up—with his former prison tucked under his arm—and walks through the sea of people. This time the shuffle on the roof moves to the edge of the wall. There above the door hang the faces of his friends staring down in wide-eyed wonder. No months of rehab. No stretching. No resistance training. Forgiveness just skips home. Here in this house packed full of overburdened moralists (with perfect legs and limbs), the paralytic is the only one who truly walks away. Which is to say, don't miss the real miracle—*forgiveness*.

I can imagine his family when he walks through his front door—maybe for the first time ever. Well, honestly, I can't imagine what that would be like. "Stunned" is not word enough to describe it. Luke says people were "struck with astonishment and glorifying God." It's overjoyed pandemonium. When things finally calm down, the former paralytic says to his speechless family, "You'll never believe what happened to me today!" They laugh as if he's trying to be amusing, but he's serious. He then says, "I was forgiven of my sins. And you can be forgiven too." There's the drama.

If you don't have the ability to explain the concept to a six-year-old kid, then you don't really understand it yourself. In other words, to simplify without distorting requires a very deep mastery of understanding of your content. And so, if you understand it then you can communicate it. If you don't understand it, you can just transfer information from your notebook to the next generation.

—R.C. SPROUL

Chapter Four

Passion and the Bland Leading the Bland

It's a sin to bore people.[78] *– R.C. Sproul*

If I were asked what in a Christian minister is the most essential quality for securing success in the winning of souls for Christ? I should reply "earnestness": and if I were asked a second or third time, I should not vary the answer, for personal observation drives to the conclusion that, as a rule, real success is proportionate to the preacher's earnestness. Both great men and little men succeed if they are thoroughly alive unto God, and fail if they are not so.[79] *– Charles Haddon Spurgeon*

The Height to Which Every Sermon Should Rise

I still remember the moment my history professor—dean of the department—slid the wooden academic chair up against his ark-like desk. The scrape of wood against the tile floor startled the entire class. Many a slumber was disturbed. Our heads simultaneously snapped up. We all watched in amazement as this refined southern scholar suddenly climbed up on his impromptu stage. The day's topic? The

---

78 Sproul, *Interview*.
79 Charles Haddon Spurgeon, *Lectures to My Students*, Complete and Un-abridged, (Zondervan: Grand Rapids, 1954), p. 145.

martyrs of Mary's reign. Nearly three hundred pastors, leaders and faithful laymen lost their lives at her cruel hands. Some suffered excruciating deaths. Their lives and deaths have been an ongoing source of inspiration for the Church. But it's easy to admire a martyr's courage when you're confident the splatter of their blood can't reach you. It was my professor's intention to draw us into range.

Up close, contemporary evangelicals are less inclined to swoon. Most of us would be scandalized to know the truth about their deaths. As to why they were willing to be burned alive. Short answer? *Words.* They objected to any explanation or wording which affirmed the "real presence" of Christ in the elements of the Lord's Table. In effect, they refused to acknowledge the efficacy of the Catholic Mass as required by Queen Mary. To be blunt, they were rounded up and murdered over a "technicality."

Many would see this as a tragic waste. A petty squabble among hard-headed opponents. Foolish even. What difference does it make whether a person confesses a real presence in the table or not? After all, they're just words. Aren't they virtually the same ideas expressed in different ways? Why not just say them? But assessments like this are naive and dangerous. The very response those with nothing to die for might offer. As J.C. Ryle put it:

> Now were the English Reformers right in being so stiff and unbending on this question of the real presence? Was it a point of such vital importance that they were justified in dying before they would receive it? These are questions, I suspect, which are very puzzling to many unreflecting minds. Such minds, I fear, can see in the whole controversy about the real presence nothing but a... strife of words.[80]

But is it really a "strife of words" if those words are everything and the difference between a damning false gospel of merit and the true Gospel of God's Grace? We'd do well to remember that a "technicality" lies at the heart of the Gospel. Paul called it the "truth" within the Gospel which distinguishes it from every other religion:

---

80   John Charles Ryle, *The Christian Leaders of the Last Century: Or England a Hundred Years Ago*, (Charles Nolan: Moscow, Idaho, 2002), p. 58.

But it was because of the false brethren who had sneaked in to
spy out our liberty which we have in Christ Jesus, in order to
bring us into bondage. But we did not yield in subjection to them
for even an hour, so that the truth of the gospel might remain
with you. (Galatians 2:4-5)

As Ryle went on to explain, capitulation on this point in any form is tantamount to denying the Gospel, "...if pursued to its legitimate consequences, [it] obscures every leading doctrine of the Gospel and damages and interferes with the whole system of the Christian truth..."[81]

Let's just say my professor cared about words. He was concerned about the *details* of the truth. So much so, he was willing to abandon his dignity in proving its importance. But what drove him was not so much the topic as much as it was our indifference toward it. He was clearly perturbed. From on top of the desk, he took issue with us. Hands tied above his head with invisible rope, standing on his tiptoes he demonstrated the effect of being "hung, drawn and quartered." I'd never given that expression much consideration. I do now. He began, "Many of the martyrs were stretched upwards and tied to posts (hung). Water was forced down their throats." Pointing to the tip of his tie with one hand he went on:

"When their bellies were finally distended—still standing in the
flames—they were cut open. Bowels roasted in a skillet right in
front of them. At some point their intestines would be fastened to
a horse's bridle. At the executioner's command, the horse would
be whipped (drawn). The result was devastating. Right before
they expired, the executioner would impale the victim finally
ending the torment of his suffering. Their remains were then cut
into pieces (quartered) and burned."

Looks of horror pervaded the classroom. Hands over mouths. Tears in eyes. The most lethargic creatures on earth—college students—had been moved. He then yelled, "Get the wood boys! Who's ready to die?"

---

81   Ryle, *The Christian Leaders of the Last Century*, p. 58-59.

By the time he concluded, his perch on the top of a desk made complete sense. The subject was worthy of the *altitude*. I got it. Everyone got it. *Words* matter. Some are worth dying over. Don't take them for granted. He stepped down, put the chair back in its place and announced, "Class dismissed." Satisfied he had executed our naiveté, he exited. It was the most effective lecture of my entire education—pre-school to grad school. I had never seen so much sincere passion utilized with such effect. Not even from behind the pulpit. Not even to this day.

In all my years as a student, no teacher before or since ever climbed up on a desk. I'm certain my GPA would have been much higher had more of them done so. Passion is potent. This is especially true in biblical preaching. It says what words cannot and reinforces the words we offer. Passion offers the listener the opportunity to feel the impact of truth. Impassioned sincerity pulls the Church right up to the fires of hell, or the blood stains on the cross, or the echo of the empty tomb. As someone said, "It turns men's ears into eyes."

A frequent criticism of biblical preaching is its unwillingness to "climb up on desks." It lacks altitude. But lifelessness makes little sense in light of the reality of the expository method—coming face to face with the mind of God in His Word. Our life is filled with "desktop" moments. Overwhelming realizations and startling insights. At least they should be. Exposition and passion are not mutually exclusive realities. One is the consequence of the other. Expositors should be the first ones climbing up on desks. Not merely for effect, but because the subject is worthy of a certain height. If more of us did, more of our people would get it. Some might even awaken.

White Belts and Shoes

I realize there's room for skepticism here. Not every display of excitement behind the pulpit qualifies as spirit-filled passion. There is a type of passion displayed in preaching which belongs in a theater. Its singsong tempo has an artificial ring. It's much more like a performance than preaching. Somewhere in the margin of the preaching notes is written, "Raise your hand here." When I hear it, I have tendency to roll my eyes.

There's another passion in preaching which belongs in the courtroom. Someone somewhere is being cross-examined. It's strident, angry and consistently piercing. Somewhere in the preaching notes is written, "Yell here… and here… and here." When I hear it, I have a tendency to turn it down.

There is yet another sort of passion in preaching which belongs on *Oprah*. It's soft, inviting and accessorized by lighting and mock turtlenecks. It's more an affable conversation than preaching. Somewhere in the preaching notes is written, "Look sincere here. Sound sophist here." For some reason when I hear it, I'm thirsty for *lattes*.

There are other species out there, but these are the easiest counterfeits to spot. Despite their tone, none of them necessarily represents real passion. Often they're strictly rhetorical devises; what they have in common is *insincerity*. No matter the form, when a preacher's passion lacks sincerity, you feel as if you just stepped onto a used car lot. It's insulting. "Persuasive speech" is misleading and dangerous when the cross is absent. Paul warned about a passion wearing white belts and shoes,

> *Therefore, since we have this ministry, as we received mercy, we do not lose heart, but we have renounced the things hidden because of shame, not walking in craftiness or adulterating the word of God, but by the manifestation of truth commending ourselves to every man's conscience in the sight of God. (2 Corinthians 4:1-2)*

On the other hand, when sincerity and passion meet—when genuine conviction results in a passionate appeal—style is immaterial. It matters not whether the preacher is dramatic, strident or conversational. You believe him. Passion is more than volume. Passion is the obvious sincerity of conviction amplified through the gifts, disposition and characteristics of the preacher. Spurgeon called it *earnestness* and understood it to be the most important element in any preacher's style. His estimation is startling, "…personal observation drives to the conclusion that, as a rule, real success is proportionate to the preacher's earnestness. Both great men and little men succeed if they are thoroughly alive unto God, and fail if they are not so."[82]

It's more an affable conversation than preaching. Somewhere in the preaching notes is written, "Look sincere here. Sound sophist here."

---

82   Spurgeon, *Lectures to My Students*, p. 145.

Earnestness is a self-evident characteristic in preaching. When I'm out of the pulpit on a given Sunday, a staff member or a guest speaker will fill the pulpit. After I return, their sermon is not the first thing I hear. Neither is it the first thing I'm listening for. What I listen for (and hear) is the impact of their sermon in the reaction of our people. Those sermons which are *earnest* leave the longest echoes. I know something of the quality of the sermon before I actually hear it.

Obviously, I've never actually heard George Whitefield preach. But, I still hear his sermons. I hear their echo hundreds of years later. He is one of the most earnest preachers in history. So earnest that he was vilified by his contemporaries for being an "enthusiast." A criticism he was happy to accept but one many other expositors are in no danger of receiving. One of Whitefield's biographers explained this quality:

> *Another leading characteristic of Whitefield's preaching was his tremendous earnestness. One poor uneducated man said of him that "he preached like a lion." He succeeded in showing people that he at least believed all he was saying, and that his heart and soul and mind and strength were bent on making them believe it too. His sermons were not like the morning and evening guns at Portsmouth, a kind of formal discharge, fired off as a matter of course, that disturbs nobody. They were all life and fire. There was no getting away from them.[83]*

In other words, it's not volume that *reaches* the people on the back row. It's gravity. Earnestness drags the back row to the front. It's compelling. It has your ear no matter how it sounds. If the preacher pauses dramatically, you hang on the next word. If he yells at the top of his lungs, you hardly notice. If he whispers, he might as well have yelled. Sincere passion has power whether it's sitting behind or standing on a desk. There's good reason. It comes from the heart and not the margins of notes.

Emotion and animation don't necessarily make for passion. This is a crucial point to grasp, especially for those preachers who might

---

83   Ryle, *The Christian Leaders of the Last Century*, p. 42.

view themselves as less than dynamic or those congregants with unrealistic expectations of their preacher. What makes for passion depends on the man, the content of the passage and the context in which the sermon is delivered.

Passion does not take on one form. Its manifestations are as diverse as the men called to preach. It may show up in an awkward silence, or a detailed explanation, or a laugh or a tear. Passion embodies the preacher. It's organic, not manufactured. Sincere passion emerges from a man confronted by the text, crushed by the cross, enraged by his sin, overjoyed by grace, abandoned to the Gospel, compelled by his calling and desperate for his people. It is a man simultaneously taking hold of a nail-pierced hand and a pulpit.

Passion is brokenness. Not a man brimming with confidence in a well-tuned manuscript or in refined oratory. It sometimes trips over its tongue and struggles for words. That is to say, it's human. Long before the sermon is preached the preacher has wept, rejoiced, grieved and repented over the truth. Through his preaching, his people are set free to do the same. His preaching is a verse-by-verse ascent of the cross. Upon hearing him, we're compelled to follow.

Dr. John Piper has been leading people up Calvary through his preaching for thirty years. He, more than any other expositor of our time, has demonstrated the possibility of combining scholarship and passion. He has exemplified the elusive balance of heart and mind through the art of exposition.

In 1979 while on sabbatical from Bethel College, he made the decision to leave the academic world and enter into the pastorate. Somewhere around midnight on October 14, 1979, he made the following entry in his journal, "I am closer tonight to actually deciding to resign at Bethel and take a pastorate than I have ever been. The urge is almost overwhelming. It takes this form: I am enthralled by the reality of God and the power of His Word to create authentic people."[84] According to his journal, the Lord's demands on his ministry were unavoidable:

---

84   John Piper, "30 Years Ago Today: How God Called John Piper to Become a Pastor", The Gospel Coalition, http//www.thegospelcoalition.org/blogs/ justintaylor/2009/10/14/30-years-ago-today-how-god-called-john-piper-to-become-a-pastor (accessed February, 2010).

I will not simply be analyzed; I will be adored... I will not simply be pondered; I will be proclaimed... My sovereignty is not simply to be scrutinized; it is to be heralded... It is not grist for the mill of controversy; it is gospel for sinners who know that their only hope is the sovereign triumph of God's grace over their rebellious will. [85]

And so John Piper stepped into the ministry and onto a desk.

---

85   Piper, John, "30 Years Ago Today: How God Called John Piper to Become a Pastor"

Dr. John Piper

Singularly Committed to "Both And"

Circa 1968, Pasadena California. Dr. Daniel Fuller is delivering a lecture on Hermeneutics to a capacity classroom at Fuller Seminary. His analytical approach to the grammatical historical method began to grate on a number of the students. As a certain eyewitness reported it, the offended were psychology majors.

The budding behaviorists could not bear the scientific and academic manner with which Dr. Fuller was addressing a specific passage. Fuller was in the process of observing the logic of a text—a certain conjunction and its syntactical relationship to the rest of passage—when they objected. "That's not where real people live! We need to have more affections, emotion and experience!" Blinded by the emphasis of their own anthropological discipline, they could not see the connection between the details of exegesis and real life. Between the "science" of interpretation and the "experience" of humanity. To put their objection in modern terms: *it was boring and irrelevant!* Where was the good stuff?

Graciously, Dr. Fuller put his book down and responded, "Why can't we be like Jonathan Edwards? A man who could write a paragraph able to bend the mind of the greatest scholar and in the next paragraph write in such a way to warm your grandmother's heart."[86]

---

86   John Piper, interviewed by author, Nashville, TN, January 26, 2010.

Clearly, this was not the first time he had faced this objection and its implied criticism. It's a rather predictable characterization. What's surprising from our vantage point is the parallel of this scene and the protests coming from the contemporary church. (The more things change, the more they remain the same.) You hear the same stale sound bites coming from all quadrants of evangelicalism. "We're not meeting the needs of real people." "Ordinary people are bored by the sermons offered in most churches." "The Church is losing its relevance." It's all the same criticism from one generation to the next.

As it turns out, an analysis offered by freshmen more than twenty years ago is just as naive as the ones we encounter today. It's full of idealism and empty of substance. They all assume the fatal "either or" position. *Either* preaching is practical, *or* it's biblical. *Either* it's passionate, or it's *cerebral*. They assume it can't be both. Really? Down here in reality it's always "both and." That is, if it's truly relevant. As has been stated elsewhere, the truest kind of relevance is the byproduct of the most rigorous sort of scholarship. By contrast, most of those saccharine applications the church is wild about today rarely have any connection to true profundity.

Back in that classroom, Dr. Fuller answered with a thoughtful "both and." He was responding to the much larger question inadvertently begged by the students. The very questions I'm putting forward in this chapter: *Are scholarship and zeal mutually exclusive realities? Can we think technically about a text and still preach with passion?*

Fuller's reply to this age-old conundrum was brilliant: *Jonathan Edwards*. Edwards' life and works prove the inextricable relationship of scholarship and worship, of exegesis and passion, of academics and application. In no way are they mutually exclusive disciplines. They are a part of the same whole. One is the natural result of the other.

By the grace and providence of God, a young freshman by the name of John Stephen Piper was in attendance to witness this exchange. Like so many before and after him, this was a question he'd been seeking to answer in his own life. As he describes it now, "I wondered was it really possible to argue with razor-sharp logic and at the same time to be blown away by what you see? To be compelled to pray, sing and do back handsprings over what you thoroughly understand?"[87]

Dr. Fuller's response initiated a moment of profound clarity in John Piper's life. In that moment, he heard described for the first time what he'd desired for his own life—"*both and.*" Internally he declared, "That's what I want to be!"[88] As history has proven, that's what he's become.

A young John Piper made his way to the library and began to rethink the goal of scholarship and deconstruct his sophomoric understanding of Edwards. Up until that moment, he had been burdened with a stereotypical opinion of the great preacher left over from high school literature classes. Edwards was assumed to be an angry prophet. His monumental contribution to American literature, *Sinners in the Hands of an Angry God*, was considered to be among the greatest scare-tactic messages of all time. The Edwards Piper eventually came to know was much different. As Dr. Piper wrote in another place, "Identifying Edwards with 'Sinners in the Hands of an Angry God' is like identifying Jesus with the woes against Chorazin and Bethsaida. This is a fraction of the whole, and is not the main achievement."[89]

As John Piper would come to realize, Edward's main achievement was not dread, but awe. The perfect balance of scholarship and affection. The more dutiful people are in their study of God in His Word, the more sincere they are in their worship of Him. One follows the other. Is it any wonder that one of the greatest theologians in the history of the Church—much less America—who possessed an unparalleled intellect is simultaneously known for the intense depth of his religious experience? This unique combination was the hallmark of Edwards' life:

> On the one hand, Edwards wanted to defend the genuine and necessary place of the affections in religious experience. On the other hand, he was relentlessly devoted to objective truth and wanted all emotion to be rooted in a true apprehension of reality and be shaped by that reality.[90]

---

87   Piper, *Interview.*

88   *Ibid.*

89   John Piper, *God's Passion for His Glory: Living the Vision of Jonathan Edwards* (Crossway: Wheaton, 1998), p. 83.

90   Piper, *God's Passion for His Glory*, p. 93.

As Edwards himself put it, "I should think myself in the way of my duty to raise the affections of my hearers as high as possibly I can, provided that they are affected with nothing but the truth, and with affections that are not disagreeable to the nature of what they are affected with."[91]

The Living Proof of "Both And"

Anyone familiar with John Piper knows his unique bond with Edwards. Besides the Bible, Edwards' writings have been a dominant influence in Piper's life. According to Piper, his ministry, preaching and writing are a working out of Edwards' vision. One of Piper's most notable works, *Desiring God*, is a common man's translation of Edwards' own magnum opus, *The End for Which God Created the World*. Countless believers have been impacted by Piper's distillation of Edwards' edict: *"God is most glorified in us when we are most satisfied in Him."*

Most of Piper's writings, regardless of the specific subject, are an extension of this fundamental conviction. It's no secret that he's written the same book a dozen times by superimposing this theocentric vision on everything from world missions to life purpose. This is in no way a criticism. I've bought and read every single one. His anthem has been an incalculable blessing to the Church in whatever form it has appeared.

There are other influences in John's life which helped prove the possibility and legitimacy of the balance between scholarship and zeal. One such influence was his father—a man whose affection for God left an indelible mark on his son. "My dad was not an intellect. But he loved God and sowed the seed of being thrilled with the glory of God."[92] Another significant and oft-cited influence in Piper's formation was C.S. Lewis. As a student at Wheaton, he heard Lewis described as a "romantic rationalist." That description resonated with John. He explained what this came to mean in his own life:

He demonstrated for me and convinced me that rigorous, precise, penetrating logic is not opposed to deep, soul-stirring feeling and vivid, lively—even playful—imagination. He was a 'romantic

---

91 Jonathan Edwards, *Some Thoughts Concerning the Revival*, in: *The Works of Jonathan Edwards*, vol. 4, ed. by C. Goen (New Haven: Yale University Press, 1972), p. 387.
92 Piper, *Interview*.

rationalist'. He combined things that almost everybody today assumes are mutually exclusive: rationalism and poetry, cool logic and warm feeling, disciplined prose and free imagination. In shattering these old stereotypes, he freed me to think hard and to write poetry, to argue for the resurrection and compose hymns to Christ, to smash an argument and hug a friend, to demand a definition and use a metaphor.[93]

Edwards, however, more than any other person was confirmation to him that analytical thinking and passionate devotion were not mutually exclusive realities. It's important to understand this when considering the impact of John Piper's preaching and writing. John was not in that library searching out either the erudition or the experience of Edwards. What he was looking for was their union.

John Piper faced the same struggle so many conscientious expositors face: how to approach the text with rigorous scholarship and adorn it with heartfelt earnestness behind the pulpit. For Piper, Edwards was proof that such a union was possible. For a new generation of preachers (and congregants), Piper is living proof of the same reality.

John's broad appeal can be traced back to this trait in his ministry. Mild charismatics, the young reformed movement, social justice-loving emergents, fundamentalists and academia all claim him. Those pushing back against the cold hardness of academics find in him an insightful and feeling friend. Those disappointed by the wanderings of popular spirituality and Christian mysticism find in him a careful and determined workman. To the former, he subtly proves the merit of biblical accuracy. For the latter, his brand of scholarship fans the flames of flickering love.

As with so many other young preachers, John Piper played a part in a similar moment of clarity in my own ministry. For countless preachers he has verified—in nearly every aspect of his life—a simple principle: scholarship and worship are not only possible but inevitably related. His own homiletic is defined by this pursuit:

---

93   John Piper, *Don't Waste Your Life* (Crossway: Wheaton, 2003), p.19.

I just want to help people be amazed at God. Stunned at God. Full of wonder at God. At the same time, my vision has a very theocentric and affectional dimension. It's not an emotion at me, or the moment, or the music. It's emotion at a real objective, clear, biblically grounded solid vision of God.[94]

Or as he explained in his timeless work *The Supremacy of God in Preaching*: "The grand design of the preacher is to restore the throne and dominion of God in the souls of men."[95]

What better example of Edwards' balance exists today than that of Dr. John Piper? He can just as easily author an intensely analytical and robust exegetical response to a current controversy[96] as he can a meditation on the benefits of Christ's death.[97] We admire him just as much for his mind as we do for his devotion. He is at one and the same time published under "Christian Living" and "Academics." He is *both and.*

"Emotion!" There I said it. Now let me explain.

"Emotion." It's a dirty word among many exegetes. Very suspect. When we hear it, we think *superficial* and *shallow*. Emotion in the pulpit makes many of us uncomfortable. I grew up in a denomination where an increase in volume usually signaled a decrease in content. It still makes me nervous. Honestly, John Piper's displays of affection have—on occasion—made me nervous. As he put it, "I can get carried away. From time to time, I have to apologize for something I say."[98] It's this occasional edge which reminds us of our own lethargy.

Ironically, even in my discussion with John he felt the need to qualify his understanding of emotion, "I use the word emotion in the best sense, not a superficial sense."[99] This raises an important question. Why is it that doctrinally minded preachers feel the need to explain the occurrence of emotion? We know the answer. In light of excesses,

---

94 Piper, *Interview*.

95 John Piper, *The Supremacy of God in Preaching* (Baker: Grand Rapids, 1990), p. 24.

96 John, Piper, *Counted Righteous in Christ: Should We Abandon the Imputation of Christ's Righteousness?* (Crossway: Wheaton, 2002).

97 John Piper, *The Passion of Jesus Christ* (Crossway: Wheaton, 2004).

98 Piper, *Interview*

99 *Ibid.*

we're concerned a display of emotion may distract from the primary goal of exposition—making the Bible clear. It's a valid concern. In many churches where emotion is emphasized in worship, its presence has little or nothing to do with a substantive response to truth.

It's counterintuitive to associate "emotion" with solid exegesis. We view it as a potential compromise of accuracy and authority. Skepticism is often warranted. But the question remains: Is there a display of passion and emotion in preaching which is actually able to reinforce exegesis and produce an appropriate response in the audience?

This need to qualify the display of emotion in preaching is at the same time *both* reasonable *and* contradictory. It's *reasonable* because of the potential for emotion to manipulate and shortcut biblically-founded convictions. As Edwards put it, our emotions must not be "disagreeable to the nature of what they are affected with." Emotion—whether in our preaching or in our response to preaching—must be based on an awareness of truth. It can't be mere sensationalism.

What better example of Edwards' balance exists today than that of Dr. John Piper? He is at one and the same time published under "Christian Living" and "Academics." He is both and.

It's *contradictory* in that we shouldn't have to justify emotion in preaching. How is it even possible to come in such close proximity to divine truths without them touching us personally, not to mention them touching our delivery? What most expositors need to explain is the absence of emotion in their preaching. One might just as easily question whether or not a person has truly exegeted a passage if its impact can't be seen in his life and delivery. Point being, the issue is not so much stylistic as it is personal.

When I asked his opinion regarding the disconnect between expositors and passion, Piper's answer was direct:

> *I don't think they have a hard time with it because they are afraid of it, but because they don't feel it. I doubt many preachers are feeling great emotion and not allowing it because they are concerned people will dislike it. They just haven't been amazed at what they see.*[100]

---

100 Piper, *Interview.*

We've proven his point every time we've "mailed" a sermon in. It can happen from time to time. (Or is that just me?) Those preaching moments when—of all those in attendance—we're the least convinced of what we're saying. The only thing we *feel* is agony. Those sermons are an offense to God. Not because of poor hermeneutics or bad mechanics, but due to the absence of earnestness. We simply don't believe and feel what we're saying on a deeply personal level. For all the times we've pressed the issue of accuracy in interpretation, we very rarely make the same demands with regard to accuracy in demeanor. There must be an "agreeable nature of our affections." There must be some impact of the truth on our lives for it to be called exposition. Right?

What Our Sermons Really Communicate

Dr. Piper goes so far as to suggest that dreariness in preaching—even the most biblical—is a subtle form of blasphemy. Our delivery can lie about God even when our words may accurately represent something God has said. Inertia has a way of denying the very truths we proclaim. He issued this warning to preachers,

> *Oh brothers, do not lie about the value of the gospel by the dullness of your demeanor. Exposition of the most glorious reality is a glorious reality. If it is not expository exultation—authentic, from the heart—something false is being said about the value of the Gospel. Don't say by your face, or by your voice, or by your life that the Gospel is not the Gospel of the all-satisfying glory of Christ. It is.*[101]

I'm not often accused of misrepresenting the truth. This is not to suggest I'm right one hundred percent of the time. No one is. There's always room for clarification and adjustment. More often than not, however, I land somewhere near the center in my interpretation and explanation. But I have inadvertently "lied about the value of the gospel" by my demeanor behind the pulpit. I can just as easily distort the truth by how I say it.

There was a time when I was accused of being lifeless and formulaic in my delivery. The criticism wasn't always delivered to my face, but it was

---

101   Mark Dever et al, *Preaching the Cross*, (Crossway: Wheaton, 2007), p. 115.

out there nonetheless. It was discussed at those legendary conferences which form around lunch tables following church services on Sunday. Those courageous (and loving) enough to discuss it with me face to face struggled to put their frustrations into words. It was amusing watching them get up the nerve to tell me I was boring. I frequently dismissed these caricatures with noble-sounding rebuttals and excuses. "You aren't serious about the Word." "You don't want to hear the truth." "It's not about being entertained." But I knew what they were trying to say. "Lead us! Show us what it means to love Christ!" These weren't nominally minded people. They loved God's Word. I knew the problem was not one of style but of devotion. The proper correction was not an adjustment in delivery but an adjustment of heart (2 Corinthians 5:12).

Spurgeon's confrontation applies here, "Are you God's servant or not? If you are, how can your heart be cold? Are you sent by a dying Savior to proclaim his love and win the reward of his wounds, or are you not? If you are, how can you wilt?"[102] The implication of Spurgeon's question(s) is devastating. There's something wrong with us if we're unmoved at the sight of the cross or the glory of God. There is no way a regenerate man can remain indifferent to biblical realities.

If our preaching is lifeless, we've got some soul searching to do. Either we're not called to preach, or we need to repent. Ours may be to lecture or teach. Teaching and lecturing are important services in the Body of Christ, but they're not the same as preaching. That is to say, you might be behind the wrong desk. Preaching is a heralding of the truth, not just an accounting of it. After all, it's called expository preaching, not expository lecturing. Piper explained the distinction:

> *Mighty in the Scriptures, aglow with the great truths of the doctrines of Grace, dead to self, willing to labor and suffer, indifferent to the accolades of man, broken for sin, and dominated by a sense of the greatness, and majesty, and holiness of God… Preaching is not conversation. Preaching is not casual talk about religious things. Preaching is not simply teaching. Preaching is the heralding of a message permeated by the sense of God's greatness and majesty and holiness. The topic may be anything under the sun,*

---

102 Spurgeon, *Lectures to My Students*, p. 161.

but it is always brought into the blazing light of God's greatness and his word.[103]

He added this within the same discussion, "But what sets the herald apart from the philosopher, and scribe, and teacher is that he is the herald of news and in our case, infinitely good news, infinitely valuable news, the greatest news in all the world."[104]

Let's say you are called to preach, but your preaching is cold. It's hard to find a pulse in your delivery. This is usually a harbinger of issues much deeper than mechanics. Your soul has been packed down hard by the traffic of ministry. You're weary. Driven to cynicism by the granite of people's indifference. The truths which once moved you no longer penetrate your own heart, much less the hearts of your people. Preaching is now an unfulfilling chore coming out in a predictable and bleak delivery of facts. With every chance to set yourself on fire, you keep on doing the same thing. It is a dangerous cycle to find ourselves in. Not only because of what it says about the condition of our souls, but primarily because of what it communicates about our God to His people or fails to communicate about Him.

Men Continually on Fire

As has been previously admitted, passion looks different in each preacher. This is a reality Piper readily acknowledges. In fact, he offered the following exhortation along these lines:

> *Please! Don't copy John Piper! You will look so stupid trying to be anybody but yourself. There is intensity, earnestness and passion in a hundred forms. You don't have to flail your arms around, or shout like I do. You have to find your own way. But, if your natural demeanor happens to be composed don't think there's no such thing as passion when it comes to your preaching.*[105]

I realize we're human. It's unrealistic to assume we'll preach from the highest elevation possible every time we preach. That's impos-

---

103   Dever, *Preaching the Cross*, p. 104-105.
104   *Ibid.*, p.115.
105   Piper, *Interview*.

sible. There are only so many desks. This isn't about superficial or disingenuous displays of emotion. It's about a consistent sincerity that survives the ups and downs of life.

As I have observed those preachers with a habitual earnestness in their delivery, I discovered a consistent feature. Those men most heartfelt behind the pulpit are earnest in every other area of their life. They not only preach with passion, they live with it. Their regular conversations about the things of God are seasoned with the same enthusiasm we observe in the pulpit. They write, pray, converse, plan and exist with a comparable intensity.

This fact was proven in an interview I conducted with author Steve Lawson, pastor of Christ Fellowship Baptist Church in Mobile, Alabama. Steve is known for "setting himself on fire." He has a way of pinning your soul to the wall through his conviction.

We met at a conference where Steve was a guest speaker. The venue allowed me to observe and interview him on the same day. Between his sessions we sat down to talk. He was physically exhausted and exhibiting flu-like symptoms. Acting from love, I sat as far away from him as I could get and still conduct the interview. Sitting opposite me across a conference table, he was the same man as he had been behind the pulpit a few moments before. His passion, though appropriate for the context of an interview, was no less palpable.

Despite his condition, not long after we began, I was "pinned down." This effect is a result of an ever-present fire, not one turned on for certain occasions. As Spurgeon once told his students, if we want to "blaze" in our discourses we must be "continually on fire" in our lives.

Passionate preachers like Piper and Lawson are men "continually on fire." Their sermons are merely those moments when the fire breaks out on the surface of their lives. Their passion is the product of a continual desperation. Which is to say, the remedy for a lifeless pulpit is not an elevation in volume but an elevation of love.

When you think about it, you'll realize it's not the style of these men we want to emulate. The fact is that the more passionate a preacher is, the harder his style is to duplicate. Their delivery is somewhat unpredictable because the various texts and topics require different levels of intensity. That element in their style we're drawn to is the "blood earnestness" of their passion. We see them preach and desire a similar type of transparency.

C.J. Mahaney is a perfect example of this reaction. In my studies I watched a video of him delivering a sermon on Christ's suffering in the garden. Before he even began to explain the text, he was in tears. I don't mean to suggest he went Tammy Faye Baker, but he was clearly broken. As he explained it, "I can't help but feel this way since I'm responsible for this scene." At that moment, his brokenness was a perfectly reasonable and naturally resulting effect of his deeply informed understanding of the Gospel's account. It was the doctrine of substitution breaking through in his heart. My thought? "Why don't I suffer the same degree of brokenness when I face those same passages?" His display did not lessen an understanding of the passage or obscure the meaning. It enhanced it. In some way, his delivery was part of the overall accuracy of the sermon.

An Enviable Blindness

Those who preach with sincere passion are stricken with an enviable kind of blindness. They can't quite see the opinions of men. They care not what people think of their display of devotion. As the Apostle explained, "For if we are beside ourselves, it is for God; if we are of sound mind, it is for you." (2 Corinthians 5:13) At the same time, their sincere passion is not showy or mere shock-value antics. When you see it, you don't see the preacher. You are as blind to him as he is to you. You see through the preacher's transparency to Christ. In hearing him you're not insulted. You're inspired.

True passion risks its own dignity to exalt Christ. True passion is a freedom from insecurity and the fear of man. It's a type of freedom people observe in a sermon on Sunday and want in their lives on Monday. Piper described this phenomenon as a liberating self-forgetfulness:

> *I just know that what I want is the gift of self-forgetfulness in what I would call a full engagement, a full passion, a full zeal with what's there in the text, and the reality of God in and through the text. I want to see Him, and know Him, be engaged*

*by Him, be thrilled by Him, say it with whatever effectiveness I
can, and let the chips fall where they will...[106]*

He offered this summary of the same idea, "It's a freedom from self-consciousness. Preaching has reached its ideal moment when I have seen and perceived and am experiencing the greatness of what I see about God in the text and am loving it."[107] Expositors should not only make sure their exegesis is thorough but also liberated. It needs to be set free.

Where's My Desk?

Ironically, one of Piper's concerns regarding passion and zeal among contemporary preachers is not just its absence. He's equally concerned about its presence. Basically, he's concerned that too many preachers are too often excited by the wrong things. The Bible bores us and strategic ministry planning excites us. It's a fair observation given the emphasis of the modern church. Honestly, how much time do we spend in our staff meetings or discussions with elders energetically putting forth and prevailing upon them with explanations of biblical truth? How often is our excitement generated by and centered around programs and plans for the ministry? As he explained it to me:

> True passion risks its own dignity to exalt Christ. True passion is a freedom from insecurity and the fear of man.

Pastors who are not driven by the Bible seem not to find any fire in the Bible. In other words, when they read the Bible on their own, they're not thrilled. When they read Barna, they get thrilled. When they read someone telling a story about how they grew a church to a thousand, they're fired up inside. I'm bored out of my mind when I read that kind of literature. I get all discouraged. I feel dead inside when I read church growth stuff. But when I read my Bible, or Edwards' exposition of my Bible, I'm bursting wanting to tell someone what I've just encountered. I write it

---

106 John Piper, "John Piper on New Word Alive and Spring Harvest," Adrian Warnock, http//www.adrianwarnock.com/2008/05/video-john-piper-interview-on-new-word (accessed May 2009).

107 Piper, *Interview.*

*down. I tweet it. I blog it. I book it and I preach it because this is
what makes me live inside. I live when I read the Bible.*[108]

This made me examine my own life. Not long after conducting
this interview, I was in my living room taking my son on in *Madden
NFL 2010* ®. We were pitted against each other in a tie game with
a few minutes to go in the fourth quarter. You know… the classic
scenario. We were all over the room jumping up and down laughing
while talking sanctified "smack." It was a blast. A great time with my
son. (He beat his father for the first time.)

Later on that same day a question occurred to me—has my son
ever seen me this excited about the Gospel? Have I ever engaged my
son in a conversation about the things of God where his dad's passion
had that type of intensity? My aim is not to condemn entertainment.
No. You can't have my game console. My point is to rebuke the lack
of joy I receive and am willing to manifest from much more thrilling
realities. Can my people discern in my preaching a reverence and love
for God? Will they this Sunday? Where's my desk?

---

108 Piper, *Interview.*

Conclusion

Improvement in the areas of *Clarity*, *Simplicity* and *Passion* has had an amazing effect in my preaching and ministry. I've been amazed at what God has done in the lives of His servant and people. As I've been transformed by an understanding of the truth, His people have been transformed in their lives. As I've been able to offer "coffee table" explanations to transcendent realities, His people have grasped them anew. As I've been unashamed in my proclamation, His people have been unashamed in their love for Him. In all this He receives the glory.

From the beginning, the goal of this project was not to become a better preacher as much as it is was to become a more useful instrument. Our aim is not to drawn attention to ourselves but to draw attention to Him through the faithful and sincere proclamation of truth. I only wanted to do a better job at making Him obvious. I think this is the goal of every faithful preacher.

For me, the means of doing that were made easier through the focus explained herein. It may not be the same for every preacher. What is true for every preacher, however, is that (ironically) you will not improve at your calling by reading a book as much as by falling on your face. Every man's journey to a liberated pulpit takes different turns. Yet, they all begin and end at the same points. They begin with a sincere desire to make much of Him. They end with a fearless energy to accomplish that desire.

I just want to help people be amazed at God. Stunned at God. Full of wonder at God. At the same time my vision has a very Theo-centric and affectional dimension. It's not an emotion at me, or the moment, or the music. It's emotion at a real objective, clear, biblically grounded solid vision of God.

—JOHN PIPER

Bibliography

Alexander, James W. *Thoughts on Preaching*. Banner of Truth Trust: Edinburgh, 1988.

Azurdia, Arturo G. *Spirit Empowered Preaching: Involving the Holy Spirit in Your Ministry*. Mentor: Great Britain, 1999.

Baucham, Voddie. "Ten Questions for Expositors", Unashamed Workman, http://www.unashamedworkman.wordpress.com/2007/04/18/10-questions-for-expositors-voddie-baucham accessed February 2009.

Begg, Allister. e-mail communication to author, May 12, 2009.

Broadus, John A. *On the Preparation and Delivery of Sermons*. 4th ed., Revised by Vernon Stanfield, Harper Collins, New York, 1979.

Chandler, Matt. "Hebrew 11", Southern Theological Seminary, http://www.sbts.edu/resources/chapel/chapel-fall-2009/hebrews-11/ accessed February 18, 2010.

Chapell, Brian. *Christ-Centered Preaching: Redeeming the Expository Sermon*. Baker: Grand Rapids, 2005.

Dever, Mark et al. *Preaching the Cross*. Crossway: Wheaton, 2007.

Dever, Mark. *What Is A Healthy Church?* Crossway: Wheaton, 2007.

DeYoung, Kevin and Kluck, Ted. *Why We're Not Emergent: By Two Guys Who Should Be*. Moody: Chicago, 2008.

Edwards, Jonathan. *Some Thoughts Concerning the Revival*, in: *The Works of Jonathan Edwards*, vol. 4, ed. by C. Goen. New Haven: Yale University Press, 1972.

Fabarez, Michael. *Preaching That Changes Lives.* Thomas Nelson: Nashville, 2002.

Ferguson, Sinclair. "Finding Your Own Voice", Unashamed Workman, http://www.unashamedworkman.wordpress.com/2007/09/18/finding-your-own-voice/ accessed February 2009.

Goldsworthy, Graeme. *Preaching the Whole Bible as Christian Scripture: The Application of Biblical Theology to Expository Preaching*. Eerdmans: Grand Rapids, 2000.

Gordon, David T. *Why Johnny Can't Preach: The Media Have Shaped the Messages*. P&R: Philipsburg, New Jersey, 2009.

Guinness, Os. *Prophetic Untimeliness: A Challenge to the Idol of Relevance*. Baker: Grand Rapids, 2003.

Heath, Chip and Heath, Dan. *Made to Stick: Why Some Ideas Survive and Others Die*. Random House: New York, 2007.

Heilser, Greg. *Spirit Led Preaching: The Holy Spirit's Role in Sermon Preparation and Delivery*. B&H: Nashville, 2007.

Henderson, David W. *Culture Shift: Communicating God's Truth to Our Changing World*. Baker: Grand Rapids, 1998.

Kaiser, Walter C., Jr. *Preaching and Teaching from the Old Testament: A Guide for the Church, Baker*. Grand Rapids, 2003.

Kaiser, Walter C., Jr. *Toward an Exegetical Theology: Biblical Exegesis for Preaching and Teaching*. Baker: Grand Rapids, 1981.

Larsen, David L. *The Anatomy of Preaching: Identifying the Issues in Preaching Today*. Baker, 1989.

Lawson, Steve. *Famine in the Land: A Passionate Call for Expository Preaching*. Moody: Chicago, 2003.

Lewis, C.S. as cited in Piper, John, *Brothers We Are Not Professionals: A Plea for Pastors for Radical Ministry*. Broadman & Holman: Nashville, 2002.

Lloyd-Jones, D. Martyn. *Preaching and Preachers*. Zondervan: Grand Rapids, 1971.

MacArthur, John, Jr. et al. *Rediscovering Expository Preaching: Balancing the Science and Art of Biblical Exposition.* Word: Dallas, 1992.

MacArthur, John. Interviewed by Author, Nashville, TN., February 6, 2009.

Mahaney, C.J. e-mail communication with author, August 4, 2009.

Martin, A.N. *What's Wrong with Preaching Today?* Banner of Truth: Carlisle, PA, 1967.

Mohler, R. Albert, Jr. *He Is Not Silent: Preaching in a Postmodern World.* Moody: Chicago, 2008.

Paggit, Doug. *Preaching Re-imagined: The Role of the Sermon in Communities of Faith.* Zondervan: Grand Rapids, 2005.

Parker, T.H.L. *Calvin's Preaching.* T & T Clark: Edinburgh, 1992.

Piper, John. "30 Years Ago Today: How God Called John Piper to Become a Pastor", The Gospel Coalition, http://www.thegospelcoalition.org/blogs/justintaylor/2009/10/14/30-years-ago-today-how-god-called-john-piper-to-become-a-pastor/ accessed February 2010.

Piper, John. *Counted Righteous in Christ: Should We Abandon the Imputation of Christ's Righteousness?* Crossway: Wheaton, 2002.

Piper, John. *Don't Waste Your Life.* Crossway: Wheaton, 2003.

Piper, John. *God's Passion for His Glory: Living the Vision of Jonathan Edwards.* Crossway: Wheaton, 1998.

Piper, John. *God is the Gospel: Meditations on God's Love as the Gift of Himself.* Crossway: Wheaton, 2005.

Piper, John. "John Piper on New Word Alive and Spring Harvest", Adrian Warnock, http://adrianwarnock.com/2008/05/video-john-piper-interview-on-new-word/ accessed May 2009.

Piper, John. *Interviewed by Author,* January 26, 2010.

Piper, John. *The Supremacy of God in Preaching.* Baker: Grand Rapids, 1990.

Piper, John. "What I Mean by Preaching", Desiring God Ministries, http://www.desiringgod.org/Blog/1792_What_I_Mean_by_Preaching/ accessed February 2009.

Reid, Robert Stephen. *The Four Voices of Preaching: Connecting Purpose and Identity Behind the Pulpit.* Brazos Press: Grand Rapids, 2006.

Renewing the Mind Ministries. "Ministry Purpose", One Place Ministries, http://www.oneplace.com/Ministries/Renewing_Your_Mind/ accessed May 2009.

Robinson, Haddon W. *Biblical Preaching: The Development and Delivery of Expository Messages.* Baker, Grand Rapids, 1980.

Ryle, John Charles. *The Christian Leaders of the Last Century: England a Hundred Years Ago.* Charles Nolan: Moscow, Idaho, 2002.

Smith, Robert Jr. *Doctrine that Dances: Bringing Doctrinal Preaching and Teaching to Life.* Broadman & Holman: Nashville, 2008.

Smith, Steve. *Dying to Preach: Embracing the Cross and the Pulpit.* Kregel: Grand Rapids, 2009.

Sproul, R.C. Interviewed by Author, May 12, 2009.

Sproul, R.C. *Chosen by God.* Tyndale: Wheaton, 1986.

Spurgeon, Charles Haddon as cited in Boice, James Montgomery, *Foundations of the Christian Faith: A Comprehensive and Readable Guide,* Revised in One Volume. IVP: Downers Grove, 1986.

Spurgeon, Charles Haddon. *Lectures to My Students,* Complete and Unabridged. Zondervan: Grand Rapids, 1954.

Stott, John R. W. *Between Two Worlds: The Art of Preaching in the Twentieth Century.* Eerdmans: Grand Rapids, 1982.

Swindoll, Chuck. *Letter to Author,* May 28, 2009.

Tozer, A. W. *The Knowledge of the Holy.* Harper Collins: San Francisco, 1961.

Vanhoozer, Kevin J. *Is There Meaning In This Text?: The Bible, the Reader, and the Morality of Literary Knowledge.* Zondervan: Grand Rapids, 1998.

White, James Emory. *A Mind for God.* IVP: Downers Grove, 2006.

Zuck, Roy B. *Basic Bible Interpretation: A Practical Guide to Discovering Biblical Truth.* Victor: Colorado Springs, 1991.

....CONTINUED ENDORSEMENTS FOR *WELL-DRIVEN NAILS*

GREAT PREACHING HAS FALLEN ON HARD TIMES TODAY. This is a must read for any laymen seeking to understand what makes a pastor an effective communicator of the truth of God's Word. Byron makes his points with passion, clarity, and humor.

—ROB IVERSON

Executive Director of Ministries, Community Bible Church, Nashville, TN
Senior Vice President Supply Chain (Former), Nestle USA
Graduate, University of Wisconsin
www.cbcnnashville.org

WELL-DRIVEN NAILS IS A TREASURE TROVE of practical advice on communicating the powerful truths of God's word. Written by a practitioner, you will find essential advice on finding your own preaching voice. You will feel like you're sitting across the table with veteran preachers and theologians such as John McArthur, R.C. Sproul, and John Piper. This book should be required reading for anyone who desires to effectively communicate God's word to others.

—DR. RICK HIGGINS

Associate Dean for Ministry Skills Development
Columbia International University, Columbia, SC

A GOOD SEMINARY WILL TEACH GOOD CONTENT, but there must be more to reach the listener. Brother Yawn hits the target with this necessary book for the Body of Christ. He writes with a passion, as I am sure he preaches. We must all find what the Lord has given us in our own mix of talents and learn to apply them. Just mimicking others or putting on Saul's armor will not carry out the Lord's will for our life. Brother Yawn uses three of my favorite preachers to bring this into focus. We must not just preach from the mind, but rather from the heart. I hope all preachers, and those who want to serve the Lord in their own unique way for His Kingdom, will read and apply this book's teaching.

—DR. JOHN HEY, MD

Teaching Elder, Grace Bible Church, Greenwood, MS
Graduate, Mississippi College; Mississippi Medical School
Founder—Greenwood Christian School
www.gracebiblechurch-greenwood.org

READING PASTOR BYRON'S EXPOSITION, I was transformed back to my own seminary graduation where Dr. Stephen Olford's commencement charge was: "Preach the word, preach the word, preach the word!" For this is all we truly have to offer those who are lost and hurting. Well-Driven Nails reminds the reader, whether young or old in the ministry, that exposition without expression may fall on deaf ears. Interviewing three of the spiritual leaders of the day, Pastor Byron provides helpful tips to keep each message biblically accurate, fresh, and relevant to today's hearer. If you have been feeling stoic in your preaching lately, application of the principles outlined in Well-Driven Nails can bring new life and power to your presentation. I recommend the book to everyone praying for success in reaching his audience.

—CHAPLAIN KEN ODOM, M.A.M.F.C.
Good News Jail & Prison Ministry
Canyon City, CO
www.goodnewsjail.org

PERHAPS THE GREATEST VALUE OF THIS BOOK is that it guides you along the path to self-discovery, to becoming the communicator God designed you to be rather than the one your professors desired you to be. I wish I had this during my seminary days!

—DR. ROBERT ISRAEL, S.T.D.
Greenville, NC
Graduate, Philadelphia College of Bible; Talbot Theological Seminary;
Bethany Theological Seminary
http://glenhavenminutes.blogspot.com

BYRON YAWN IS MY PASTOR, MY BOSS, MY FRIEND. And by "friend" I mean more than a buddy; I mean the type of friend that can tell you the hard truth you can't even tell yourself, but with the grace and understanding of one who's fought the same battles. That said, Well-Driven Nails is the heart of a friend sharing his heart to see you grow.

This book isn't just about preaching...it's about life. The concept of finding your voice is really about confronting the idols we bow to in place of Christ. Byron's heart is to see his audience liberated from the bondage of trying to please others to be free to proclaim the only message that counts...the gospel of Jesus Christ.

—DANNY WOODS
Family and Children's Pastor
Community Bible Church
Nashville, TN
Graduated, The Master's College
www.cbcnashville.org

PREACHERS LIVE AMID AN UNRELENTING PRESSURE. On the one hand there is the desire to be a faithful steward of God's gifting and calling, and on the other hand the realization that we are weak, sinful and rather unspectacular. How do we deal with this? Do we quit? Despair? Copy some other preacher who is successful? Byron Yawn has realized, analyzed, and is dealing with it. Ever the faithful pastor, he wants to help us with it too. This book is as refreshing as it is engaging and helpful.

—ERIK RAYMOND
Pastor of Preaching
Omaha Bible Church South Campus,
Omaha, NE
Blogger-Irishcalvinist.com

THE PERSONAL EFFECT OF THE WRITING of *Well-Driven Nails: The Power of Finding Your Own Voice* has had a monumental impact on Byron's congregation. We have been blessed, challenged, and stretched to a greater love for God and a broader devotion to Christ as we have watched our Pastor's faith deepen as he wrote this invaluable piece of work. It is Byron's prayer and our hope that local congregations within the body of Christ will be challenged as we have been challenged.

—GUY HASKINS
Chairman of the Elders
Community Bible Church
Nashville, TN

FOR MORE INFORMATION ABOUT
BYRON YAWN AND COMMUNITY BIBLE CHURCH

www.cbcnashville.org